A Self-study Guide to Teaching Competencies in Early Childhood Education

Mary Eitingon Kasindorf

COMPETENCIES

Humanics Learning
P. O. Box 7447
Atlanta, Ga. 30309

Humanics Learning is an imprint of Humanics Publishing Group

Second Printing 1990

PRINTED IN THE UNITED STATES OF AMERICA
ISBN 0-89334-024-3

Library of Congress Card Catalog Number: 79-87586

CONTENTS

COMPETENCY GOAL I

COMPETENCY GOAL II

COMPETENCY GOAL III

COMPETENCY GOAL IV

COMPETENCY GOAL V

COMPETENCY GOAL VI

Preface

The first edition of this training guide was based on my experiences as a mentor in the Head Start Satellite Child Development Associate Program at Empire State College, State University of New York. The Head Start Early Childhood Specialists, the students, and I used the competency areas of the Child Development Associate Program as a frame of reference to identify and list those aspects of a preschool program that would indicate to a trainer or teacher supervisor that it was an environment that would support and enhance children's growth and development. The students in the CDA program used the different aspects of each competency as a way of evaluating their own skills and training needs. By reading the list of competencies, students could see which aspects of their own teaching met the standards of quality programming and also could identify the areas in which they required further information and training. They could use the identified resources and learning activities as part of their training program.

The Child Development Associate Program has grown and changed over the years. This second edition has been updated to conform to the changes in the competencies and functional areas. New resources have also been identified. I hope that this new edition will help the many students and teachers working in Head Start Programs, center-based day care programs, and nursery schools to become the most effective and caring teachers they can be.

I am most grateful for the information and materials provided by the CDA National Credentialing Program upon which this guide has been based.

Introduction

The competencies identified by the CDA National Credentialing Program are applicable to all of us in the field of Early Childhood Education and we should all be aware of what constitutes a good early childhood education program. Even though each of us will work with young children in our own way, there is a common basis of competency that we should expect of ourselves and of all teachers. We each have specific strengths and skills, and should use them effectively to develop others.

When you use this guide you will find that it is divided into the six competency areas and thirteen functional areas of competence as identified by the CDA National Credentialing Program for center- based teachers of young children.* The competency areas are organized as follows:

A. Short general explanation and theoretical background.

B. Brief introduction and description of the related functional areas, followed by a checklist of teacher and child behavior and activities that indicate competence in the area.

C. List of readings related to the functional area which the reader can use to deepen understanding and awareness of the area.

D. Learning activities which the reader can use to develop skills in the practical applications of theory related to the competency.

As you work through the learning activities - developing curriculum materials, bibliographies, observational records, etc. - you will be developing materials which also can be used in assembling the portfolio and documenting competence for the CDA credential. These materials could be: photographs of children using teacher-made materials and working in a classroom planned and organized by teachers, lesson plans, written observations and records of children's reactions and behavior, children's art products, written record of children's stories, songs, etc., and reports of parent activities and their involvement in the program. These materials and activities can be produced independently or in connection with fellow staff members and/or under the supervision of early childhood specialists. Materials and activities to be used with children and parents should be evaluated either by fellow staff or early childhood specialists.

If you wish to use this guide for self-study and training, you can use the space to the left of each item of teacher activity, reading resources, and individual learning activity, to note whether these are areas, methods, etc., in which you feel you are functioning effectively or whether you wish to change or improve. You can also indicate if you have completed a reading or learning activity.

*The CDA National Credentialing Program, 1718 Connecticut Avenue NW, Washington, DC 20009.

It has been my experience that some general readings serve as a good introduction to the six basic areas of competence, specifically, readings about general early childhood programs and child development before Competency II (to advance Physical and Intellectual Competence) and readings in development of personality before Competency III (to support Social and Emotional Development and Provide Positive Guidance and Discipline).

It has also proved helpful for students to learn about patterns and problems of family living, child rearing, etc., before working in the area of Establishing Positive and Productive Relationships with Families (Competency IV). It is best to look through the bibliography in each section and select with the help of a trainer, fellow worker, or early childhood specialist books that you will enjoy reading and find useful in your work in the classroom. After completing the selected readings, choose learning activities that make sense to you for use in your own centers and programs, and think up new activities to share with fellow workers in the field. Remember that the plans, materials, etc., produced in completion of the activities also provide evidence of your competence in each area for center-based teachers. Also listed in each functional area are the competencies for teachers working towards a Bilingual Specialization.

Any activity that helps you become an active participant in a teaching-learning situation is an activity that helps both you and the children grow and develop. Reading over the guide, you will find that you are already involved in the behavior that supports children's growth. It is reassuring to know when we are on the right track and useful to know how we can improve and refine our skills. In working with the CDA programs and the students, I have probably learned more than I will ever teach anyone else about good preschool education. If we all move forward together, our children will benefit. The world is becoming more and more complex, and we cannot afford to lose the good ideas, creativity, and capacity for constructive thought of any human being. Who can identify the benefactors of mankind when they are two and three years old? Only if we value each child as deeply as we would be valued ourselves can we ensure that they will grow up to help us all, and to reach their goal of responsible self-fulfillment.

Our children deserve the very best we have to offer them - our knowledge, skills, love, and concern. Although we have deserved the same of others in the past, many of us have not received the best care and training. It is important that we give such care to our children.

I would like to express my gratitude to Dr. Rhoada Wald, initiator and coordinator of the Head Start Satellite at Empire State College, State University of New York; Renee Kaplan, Adjunct Mentor of the Head Start Satellite; Linda Papaleo, secretary; and the Suffolk County Head Start Early Childhood Specialists Ethel Cross, Helene Wein, and Larry Wilkerson, for help in developing the original edition of this book. My affection and gratitude go out to all the students who participated in the CDA training program. Together we all learned how to serve our children better than we had before.

While there have been some changes in the functional areas to reflect our increased awareness of the many aspects of young children's lives that affect their development, the basic competencies have remained essentially the same. They continue to relate directly to the teacher's ability to provide quality programs and growth-enhancing environments for young children. Using these competencies as a frame of reference has helped me as I have worked with staff, students, and families in many different early childhood settings.

I hope this revised edition will continue to help students and teachers who wish to work with young children and complete the CDA credentialing program.

I would like to thank my many wonderful colleagues and teachers, especially Mary Bondarin, Chief Bureau of Child Development and Parent Education in the New York State Department of Education; the late Dr. Annie Louise Butler, first chairperson of the CDA Consortium; my parents; my husband; and my children, who all helped me grow in understanding the complexities of learning, loving, and growing.

A look at your classroom...

Index of Competency Areas*

Competency Goal I - *To establish and maintain a safe, healthy learning environment*

Functional Areas:
1. Safe
2. Healthy
3. Learning Environment

Competency Goal II - *To advance physical and intellectual competence*

Functional Areas:
4. Physical
5. Cognitive
6. Communication
7. Creative

Competency Goal III - *To support social and emotional development and provide positive guidance and discipline.*

Functional Areas:
8. Self
9. Social
10. Guidance and Discipline

Competency Goal IV - *To establish positive and productive relationships with families.*

Functional Areas:
11. Families

Competency Goal V - *To ensure a well-run, purposeful program responsive to participants' needs.*

Functional Areas:
12. Program Management

Competency Goal VI - *To maintain a commitment to professionalism*

Functional Areas:
13. Professionalism

*Developed by the Child Development Associate National Credentialing Program, Washington DC. The name Child Development Associate, the anacronym CDA, is the registered trademark of the National Credentialing Program. Their use does not imply the sponsorship of the Council for Early Childhood Professional Recognition or any of its employees.

Competency Goal I

TO ESTABLISH AND MAINTAIN A SAFE, HEALTHY LEARNING ENVIRONMENT

Functional Areas:
1. Safe
2. Healthy
3. Learning Environment

In order for adults and young children to work together in a learning environment for their mutual growth and benefit, teachers and adults concerned with the education of young children must provide an environment in which children are safe, are not exposed to anything that would endanger their health, and materials and equipment are so arranged that by living and working in the classroom, children learn many things they need to know about the world. A well-organized learning environment is a basic and essential teaching tool for any competent teacher. Just by its organization, we teach children many cognitive skills, encourage their development of large and small muscle skills, and lay a foundation for the development of their positive self concept by fostering independence and a sense of self. In a well-organized classroom, we can supply the materials for learning without having to place ourselves between the children and their learning experiences. As Madame Montessori said, "Children are asking us,'Help me to do it myself'." [1]

COMPETENCY GOAL I
FUNCTIONAL AREA 1 - SAFE

The first responsibility of those who care for young children is to provide a safe environment. When we are sure that there are no physical dangers to the children in their rooms and playgrounds, we can relax and concentrate on encouraging children's full and complete development. Children will be aware of our concern and sense that they are physically safe and they will relax, explore, and enjoy their environment as completely as possible.

---

[1] Montessori, Maria, Dr. Montessori's Own Handbook, Schocken Books, N. Y., p. 11, Introduction by N. M. Rambush

1

As teachers, we should be aware of all that is involved in maintaining a safe environment. We should also understand that part of this responsibility involves making the other adults who work in the program and in the community equally aware of safety for young children and helping children themselves notice safety factors in their daily living and learning for which they can reasonably be expected to assume some responsibility.

Children must be kept safe from gross physical harm. If we can't protect them from hazards that result in real physical or mental harm, we do not have the right to take care of them. Children must be protected in situations where the consequences of unsafe behavior are completely beyond their understanding. For example, we may tell children not to run in the road because they could get hurt; but they really don't understand that "hurt" can mean much more than the scrapes and bumps they may normally experience. Therefore, we must supervise and protect them with adequate fencing, etc., so there is no possibility of running across a street until they are old enough to understand the seriousness of their actions. In the meantime, by example, instruction, and dramatic play, we help children learn how to deal constructively with danger - for example: holding hands as we cross a street, meeting crossing guards, pretending to be policemen, etc.

Usually, children are ready to listen to reasonable limitations and clear instructions when they sense that adults are concerned and care about them. The four-year-old who announces, "My Mommy won't let me ride my trike in the street," is really saying, "My Mommy cares enough to keep me safe."

Anything that results in physical damage to children and that might have been prevented constitutes an inexcusable lack of care. The fault may be in inadequate training of staff, low standards for health care, or poor supervision by administrators. It does not matter. We must all work to eliminate preventable hazards. As anyone who works with young children knows, things always "happen". I have seen a child turn on his ankle and hit his head on a stone on the ground in front of me. Such accidents happen, and they are part of living. However, falling off a poorly maintained, incorrectly-sized piece of playground equipment does not need to happen. In both cases, as teachers we must provide support and care for the child. We should be aware of first aid and availability of treatment. We must be calm, in control, and set an example of responsible behavior. Even in the case of an injury, children can learn that the damage is not permanent, that grownups can help, and that they themselves can help each other and even develop some ideas of what they should and should not do.

The following checklist can help you to evaluate your classroom in the area of safety.

Functional Area I

Safe Checklist*

In order to maintain safe classrooms and playgrounds, we as teachers should know and practice the following aspects of a safe environment:

——1. Standards of fire prevention are met (firedoors clear, fire extinguishers properly maintained, etc.). Fire drill routines are known to staff and practiced according to regulation.

——2. We are aware of common sources of accidents:

☐ Block buildings are not allowed to be built too high, children do not climb on furniture, and broken equipment is removed from the children's reach and repaired.

☐ Equipment is neither too large nor too small for children.

☐ Electrical outlets are protected.

☐ Use of electrical equipment is always supervised.

☐ Playground area has fences and children are kept safe from traffic, etc. Surfaces under playground equipment are designed to prevent injuries from sand, rubberized surface, etc.

☐ Building provides adequate protection from intruders; entrances and exits are supervised.

☐ Heating equipment is properly enclosed to protect children.

☐ There is safety equipment on buses - seat belts, lights, bus monitor, radio communication, first aid kit, and fire extinguishers. Copies of permission slips for trips and treatment are in the bus for trips outside the local area.

☐ Children are never left without adult supervision indoors or outdoors.

☐ Adults are aware of where children are at all times - who picks children up from school, etc.

——3. We know how to get help quickly in an emergency - hospital, police, fire, other staff members. Children's health and emergency records are maintained.

——4. Permission slips are given to parents and are signed so children may take trips away from the school/center.

——5. Indoor furniture and outdoor equipment are maintained in good repair.

——6. Safety procedures on the bus are identified and understood by children and adults, i.e. children know they must have their seatbelts fastened before the bus starts.

If we are working towards a Bilingual Specialization, we should:

——7. Provide all safety information in both languages.

——8. Label all emergency equipment and exits in both languages.

*This checklist may be copied for your portfolio.

Resources

The following resources contain information and ideas that should be helpful in setting up and maintaining a safe environment in which young children can live and learn.

Green, Martin. *A Sigh of Relief - A First Aid Handbook for Childhood Emergencies.* New York: Bantam Books.

Marotz, L., Rush, J. and Cross, M. *Health Safety and Nutrition for the Young Child.* Albany, New York: Delmar, 1985.

NAEYC *Resource Guide #789 Facility Design for Early Childhood Programs.* NAEYC. Washington DC.

Sanoff, H. and Sanoff, J. *Learning Environments for Children - Shaping Activity Areas.* Atlanta: Humanics Limited, 1981.

Sanoff, H. *Planning Outdoor Play.* Atlanta: Humanics Limited, 1982.

Segal, M. and Tomasello, L. *Nuts and Bolts - Organization and Management Techniques for an Interest-Centered Classroom.* Atlanta: Humanics Limited, 1981.

Learning Activities

Choose some of these activities to help you apply what you have learned through your readings and experience. Think of and record at the end of this section other learning activities that may help you work in this area.

——1. Make an outline of safety goals needed to maintain a safe learning environment for young children and identify the reasons for each goal.

——2. List some learning objectives relating to safety for the preschool child, such as identifying and practicing ways of walking on a trip, safe behavior on the bus, etc. List ways of helping children understand these objectives.

——3. Make up learning activities that will help preschool children develop understanding of self-care skills related to their own safety. Note and record children's reactions to these activities. Are they developing some awareness of their own responsibilities for their own safety?

——4. Develop a guide for staff behavior in relationship to children's safety, such as arrangements for supervision, permission for children to be taken from school, center, etc.

——5. Design materials and activities to help teachers carry out their responsibilities at school in maintaining children's safety - a chart showing emergency exits, bus supervision, and checking and recording who picks up children at dismissal.

——6. Design materials and activities to help parents carry out their responsibilities at home in maintaining their children's safety, such as charts showing adequate storage of poisons, dangerous household plants, etc.

——7. Make up a booklet for parents of preschool children, to explain safety at an adult level of understanding.

——8. Make up a booklet for preschool children, to explain safety at their level of understanding.

——9. Collect materials to help parents deal with safety issues in the community - i.e. not talking to strangers, etc.

If you are working towards a Bilingual Specialization:

——10. Make up safety guides for parents and staff in both languages.

——11. Develop learning activities connected with safety in both languages, checking to see that children are developing understanding of the concepts of safety we want them to learn: wear your seat belt in the car, don't talk to strangers, don't put plants and out door things into your mouth.

Other Related Learning Resources and Activities
(Fill in your own resources.)

_____

_____

_____

_____

_____

_____

_____

_____

_____

_____

_____

_____

_____

COMPETENCY GOAL I
FUNCTIONAL AREA 2 - HEALTHY

Maintaining a healthy environment for young children is as important as maintaining a safe environment. As teachers, we must be aware of good health standards for young children. These involve standards of cleanliness, staff health, appropriate temperature, light and an absence of hazardous materials. It is important to be aware of children's physical health, including immunization, indicators of children's health, and of first aid skills.

Another major aspect of a healthy environment is the nutritional program. Whether the early childhood program offers snacks or school meals, as teachers we should be aware of what constitutes a balanced diet. We should know how to present nutritious foods to children by using these foods in ways that encourage the development of good eating habits and by eliminating foods low in nutritional value. Use the following checklist to help you evaluate health in your classroom.

Functional Area 2

Healthy Checklist*

In order to support and foster good health in young children, teachers, should know and maintain the following aspects of a healthy environment:

——1. Light, heat, and air are kept at best possible levels for the health of children and adults.

——2. Toilets are cleaned and disinfected regularly.

——3. Children's toothbrushes and paste, hairbrushes, etc., are properly stored. Each brush is individually protected and labeled. Individual tooth pastes are used.

——4. Children's cots and bedding are marked with their names and stored to prevent the spread of any infection.

——5. Laundering arrangements for children's bedding are made.

——6. Housekeeping area utensils and doll bedding are washed on a weekly basis; by children if possible.

——7. Rooms are swept, floors and tables washed, playground is cleared of litter on a regular basis.

——8. We are aware of each child's medical and health history and special needs.

——9. We are aware that all children are properly immunized for their age and are in good health.

——10. Permissions and records for giving children medication are carefully and consistently maintained.

——11. We are aware of appropriate clothing for children - adequate protection against dampness, cold, and heat.

——12. We are aware of basic nutritional requirements of children in preschool programs. We can identify good cooking experiences and children's snacks. Menus for meals and snacks are drawn from the basic food groups required for balanced nutrition.

——13. We are aware that good standards for food preparation must be met, such as use of dishwashers, proper dishwashing arrangements, or disposable plates and utensils.

——14. Daily program allows for adequate nap or quiet time in a full-day program, allowing children to relax with toy or blanket. Children are not pressured to sleep but helped to develop habits of relaxation.

——15. Parents are helped to be aware of need for adequate outer clothing to take advantage of weather experience outdoors.

*This checklist may be copied for your portfolio.

——16. Parents are made aware of need for changes of clothing.

——17. We recognize unusual behavior or symptoms which may indicate a need for health care.

☐ There are people in each center who have first aid training.

☐ We are aware of childhood illnesses and symptoms of ill health.

☐ Teachers can do routine daily health screening or are aware that someone on the staff does this screening.

☐ Teachers observe children to see if they are listless, sleepy, cranky, crying, pale, complain of pain, have skin rashes, untreated cuts, sores, etc., unusual injuries, swelling, lumps, changes in normal behavior, eye discoloration.

☐ We are aware of signs of child abuse and maltreatment.

☐ We are aware of the need for dental, vision, and hearing screening, and regular health checkups, including immunizations.

☐ Teachers bring the needs for such examinations to the attention of appropriate staff members and parents.

☐ We are aware of common emotional problems and special needs.

☐ We are aware of common learning disabilities.

☐ We share information about the children's health and developmental needs with children's parents or guardians and help them find and work with specialists and special resources when needed.

——18. Daily program provides adequate opportunity for large muscle activity for all children.

——19. Provision is made for independent use of toilet facilities in terms of correct height, availability of paper towel, soap, etc.

——20. Boys and girls use the facilities jointly. Children do not have to wait to use facilities if waiting can be avoided.

——21. Children are helped to learn good health habits: washing hands after toileting, before eating, etc.

If we are working towards a Bilingual Specialization, we need to:

——22. Share with parents all information about health and basic nutrition in both languages.

——23. Explain health requirements and reasons for these requirements in both languages, incorporating families' cultural practices into medically accepted standards.

Resources

The following resources contain information and ideas that should be useful in helping you learn how to set up and maintain a healthy environment in which young children can live and learn.

Abbott-Shim, M., Ph.D. and Sibley, A., Ph.D. *Child Care Inventory and Administration Manual.* Atlanta: Humanics Limited, 1986.

Kendrick, A, Kaufman R. and Messenger K.P. *Healthy Young Children: A manual for early childhood programs.* NAEYC. Washington DC, 1987.

McCracken, J.B. *Keeping Healthy: Parents, Teachers and Children.* NAEYC. Washington DC, 1988.

Goodwin,M.Pollen G. *Creative Food Experiences for Children.* (rev.ed) Center for Science in the Public Interest, Washington DC, 1980.

Wanamaker, N., Hearn, K & Richarz,S., *More Than Graham Crackers: Nutrition Education and Food Preparation with Young Children.* NAEYC. Washington DC.

Warren, J, *Supersnacks.* Everett, Washington: Warren Publishing House, 1982.

Learning Activities

The plans and materials produced in completing these activities also provide evidence of your competence in this area. Choose some of these activities to help apply what you have learned through your readings and experience.

——1. Outline health goals for a preschool program with explanation for each goal.

——2. Organize, list, and/or design learning activities to help preschool children develop un derstanding and self-help skills related to their own health - washing hands after toileting, wearing the right clothing for the weather.

——3. Organize materials and plan activities for use by parents in maintaining their children's health. These can involve a wide variety of things, such as dental care, good nutrition, hand-washing routines, appropriate clothing, etc.

——4. Using readings or discussions with health care personnel, list common symptoms of emotional disturbances, learning disabilities, and symptoms of abuse and maltreatment to use in evaluating children's health.

——5. Develop a list of physical symptoms for staff to be note during routine screening of all children.

——6. Find or make up booklets for parents of preschool children to explain health and safety as it concerns their children.

——7. Find or make up a booklet for preschool children to explain health at their level of un-derstanding.

If you are working towards a Bilingual Specialization:

——8. Develop materials for parents and children in both languages.

——9. Support non-English-speaking parents and guardians in meeting children's medical and health needs, working with specialists when needed.

Other Related Learning Resources and Activities
(Fill in your own resources.)

_____

_____

_____

_____

_____

_____

_____

_____

_____

_____

_____

_____

_____

_____

_____

COMPETENCY GOAL I
FUNCTIONAL AREA 3 - LEARNING ENVIRONMENT

There are certain elements and aspects of room arrangement, storage of materials, etc., that help to support children's emotional, social, intellectual, and physical growth. The classroom does not have to be new, and the equipment and materials do not have to be elaborate. However, the room should be orderly and invite children to explore and use its contents. This should also be true of the outside learning areas.

> # Functional Area 3
> # Learning Environment Checklist*

Teachers should be aware of how to maintain the classroom and the outdoor learning space so the following indications of a good learning environment are present:

—1. Indoor classroom space provides areas for:

Dramatic play	Music and movement
Food service (if necessary) and cooking	Woodworking
Block building	Waterplay**
Language arts	Sandplay**
Manipulative materials	Resting
Creative art materials	Toileting
Science	

The equipment is used regularly so children have the opportunity to work in all the above areas.

—2. Outdoor learning space provides areas for:

☐ Wheel toys - smooth riding surface
☐ Climbing
☐ Large construction activities including materials children can use to construct their own environment
☐ Water play
☐ Sand play
☐ Multi-level space for play
☐ Outdoor art area
☐ Outdoor science area
☐ All equipment is the right size for children to use and is used regularly.

—3. Space is organized so that areas both indoors and out are recognizable and make sense to children and adults working together.

---

*This checklist may be copied for your portfolio.
**When space is limited, we may have to choose either a water play area or a sand play area, but children should have the opportunity to play with one or the other.

——4. The placement of centers of interest in the classroom is planned to encourage friendly interactions between children.

☐ Quiet areas involving language arts, science, math, etc., are next to each other where possible.

☐ Dramatic play/housekeeping and block areas are near each other so that dramatic play in each area can be related and can develop in complexity.

☐ Art materials and water play area have water available, if possible.

☐ Woodworking area is located out of traffic lanes, possibly near blocks or paint area.

☐ Children do not have to pass through one area to get to other areas in ways that may be disruptive.

——5. Furniture, equipment, and materials are arranged in ways that are understandable to the children and encourage sorting, categorizing, and self-help skills.

——6. Housekeeping/dramatic play area is set off from the rest of the room and is properly equipped:

☐ Area is set up attractively at start of every day with child-size equipment - bed, sink, stove, cabinets, refrigerator.

☐ There is storage for dress-up clothes identified by pictures and names.

☐ There is a selection of regular small pots, pans, dishes, and assorted kitchen utensils (blunt knives only); storage is marked by pictures and words.

☐ Dolls are integrated by sex, age, race, and culture and come in different sizes.

☐ Dress-up clothes and doll clothes have simple fastenings that teach self-help skills and that a child can handle; storage is marked by pictures and words.

☐ Cleanup equipment is easily reached and child-sized.

☐ There is an assortment of bedding, curtains, rugs, cushions, etc., that can be used to support dramatic play activities.

☐ Dramatic play materials for specific role play, i.e. nurses' and doctors' equipment and uniforms, beauty parlor and barber equipment are there for children to use. These are stored in separately marked containers.

☐ Pictures related to children's activities and those of their families and cultures, are attractively mounted and hung in the dramatic play area at child's eye level, and covered with clear plastic and changed regularly.

——7. The block area is well stocked and orderly:

☐ There is enough space for children to build out of traffic lanes.

☐ There is a large variety of unit blocks.

☐ There is a large variety of hollow blocks.

☐ There are enough shelves for the unit blocks marked for storage by shape and size.

☐ There is a variety of block accessory toys with clearly marked storage labeled by pictures of toys and names.

☐ Floor storage space has been marked for large accessory toys and large blocks.

☐ Pictures relating to children's activities in the block area are attractively mounted, covered with contact paper, and hung at children's eye level and changed regularly.

——8. Language arts area contains the following:

☐ Varied, appropriate, multi-cultural selection of books.

☐ Book selection which changes at regular times to match children's interests and cultures.

☐ Books, displayed and stored in shelves, which can be reached and used by children independently.

☐ Rugs, mats, rocking chair space, etc., for sitting and looking at books.

☐ Pictures on wall at children's eye level, where possible, to stimulate interest and discussion in books, changed regularly.

☐ Area set aside for quiet learning.

☐ Paper, pencils, and materials for copying and tracing of shapes, letters and numbers when children are ready for such activities.

☐ Audio-visual materials for listening and looking skills arranged to encourage children's independent use.

——9. Manipulative materials and equipment, a vital part of any learning environment, are carefully organized in a special area:

☐ Materials are stored in individual storage containers labeled with name and picture of the toy or material.

☐ Containers are large enough to hold all parts of each toy easily so children can put pieces away independently.

☐ Math materials are grouped together or there is a specific math area.

☐ There are games and toys for individual children to use independently: stacking toys, pegboards, beads, etc.

☐ There are games and toys for small groups of children to use.

☐ There are puzzles of varying degrees of difficulty.

☐ There is a variety (at least 6) of put-together toys that are changed with interest.

☐ There are materials to use to copy patterns - mosaics, table blocks, tile, etc.

☐ There are wooden and textured letters and numbers to feel, copy, etc.

☐ Adequate mat or table space is provided for individual children to use.

——10. Creative arts area is organized so that children are encouraged to use materials as independently as possible.

☐ Adequate table and easel space is available for children to work.

☐ Tables and floor have protection when needed.

☐ Cleanup equipment is easily reached and is child-sized.

☐ Smocks for children are available for them to use independently.

☐ There is a variety of paper: size, shape, and color, all sorted and easily stored so children can take paper independently.

☐ Collage materials are varied, sorted, and stored neatly in easily reached containers.

☐ Scissors are available - left- and right-handed, in a convenient container.

☐ Variety of pastes are available with some sort of individual containers for children to use independently.

☐ Printing materials are available - sorted and stored neatly.

☐ Crayons are available for all children, pieces that are too small to use are removed.

☐ There is a place for hanging or storing art projects to dry.

☐ Art projects are labeled with children's names and the dates in upper lefthand corner when possible.

☐ Variety of paints are available in all basic colors.

☐ Easel is set up with all primary colors and paper and brushes *everyday*.

☐ Clay is available with adequate moisture protection, in individual balls easily reached by children.

☐ Clayboards, water containers, and utensils to use with clay are available.

—11. The science area must be interesting and varied to attract children's attention.

☐ It is easily reached by children and visible in the room but not where traffic will result in breakage, etc.

☐ Materials are neatly and attractively arranged.

☐ Materials are changed regularly to match children's interests.

☐ There are live animals and growing plants.

☐ There are collections, labeled and interesting to children. Teachers have and use a collection of pictures relating to the items in the science area.

☐ There are materials relating to electricity sorted and stored in a container accessible to children for independent use if children are old enough.

☐ There are materials relating to magnetism sorted and stored and accessible to children for their independent use.

☐ There is an area available and equipped for cooking activities; this area may also be set up as needed.

☐ There are doors or windows for observations of weather, etc.

☐ There are books available to the children relating directly to the items in the science area.

—12. In the woodworking area, there are provisions made for:

☐ An area located out of traffic areas.

☐ An area protected by low room dividers, etc.

☐ An area easily and constantly supervised.

☐ Clearly marked accessible tool storage, sturdy workbench, small sizes of regular tools, i.e. hammers and saws.

☐ An adequate supply of soft wood in a variety of sizes, and accessible storage for the wood.

☐ Accessory materials children can use to decorate their work; sorted and stored so children can reach them, with assorted wood shapes, bottle caps, hooks, paper rolls, rubber bands, a supply of easy-to-use nails with wide heads, etc.

—13. In the sand play area, there are:

☐ Alternative materials available if sand use is limited.

☐ Sand play table (may be outdoors only if space is limited).

☐ Containers for mini sand environment (wash basins or pans) with sorted materials to use individually or by two children at a time.

☐ A variety of sand toys emphasizing differences in size, shape, and volume, stored separately in clearly marked, easily reached containers.

☐ Accessory materials and toys to encourage dramatic play (small cars, animals, people) clearly marked and easily reached.

☐ Cleanup materials easily reached and child-sized - dust pan, brooms, etc.

——14. The water play area is carefully organized. There are:

☐ Large and small water play containers for individual and group use.

☐ A variety of equipment to use with water, encouraging experimentation with pressure, movement, volume, air, weight, etc.

☐ Clearly marked storage for the play equipment easily reached by children and which allows for drainage when necessary.

☐ Cleanup equipment is easily reached and child-sized - buckets, sponges, etc.

——15. There is space for movement and music activities provided by a separate area or by rearranging the room on occasion. The following is included in the classroom:

☐ Instruments displayed and stored so that children can use them independently.

☐ Space and equipment available for independent listening (possibly in language arts area).

☐ A record player and records for group music activities.

☐ Records for group and individual use including movement, storytelling songs, and classical and folk music selections.

——16. Large muscle activity area, indoor and/or outdoor, are provided.

☐ Areas which can be used daily.

☐ Enough space for wheel toys, paved if possible.

☐ Sand/water or digging area, to be used daily.

☐ Storage containers for sand and water toys on-site and also easily removed for safekeeping.

☐ Easily reached storage for wheel toys, hollow blocks, etc., so as to encourage independent use and storage by children.

☐ Swings with soft or protected seats - swing area separated from the rest of the playground.

☐ Soft surface under swings and slide.

☐ Different levels on which children may play and climb.

☐ A planting or garden area with necessary supplies.

☐ A variety of building materials for children to construct their own environments: tires, planks, barrels, large hollow blocks.

☐ Complete fencing for the outdoor area so the boundaries are clear to children and they are safe to move about anywhere within the area.

——17. In a learning environment that supports growth of young children, the classroom is organized so that children can develop self-help skills in caring for their own physical needs.

☐ All classroom equipment and materials that children can use independently are stored at child height.

☐ All equipment for storing children's own spare clothing, outdoor clothes, and bedding is clearly marked by correctly printed name and by some appropriate symbol or sign.

☐ Space and time are allotted for children to try to dress themselves.

☐ Identifying name tag, and sign or symbol, are the same for child's individual storage areas, work storage area, transportation tag, attendance chart, and work chart, etc.

If you are working towards a Bilingual Specialization, you need to:

—18. Provide a variety of bi-cultural materials, pictures, toys, books, and games in each area of the classroom and outdoors.

Reading Resources

The following resources contain information and ideas that will be helpful in setting up and maintaining a good learning environment for young children.

Indoor and Outdoor Learning Environments

Baker, K.R. *Lets Play Outdoors.* NAEYC. Washington DC.

Commins, Elaine. *Early Childhood Activities.* Atlanta: Humanics Limited, 1982.

Commins, Elaine. *Lessons from Mother Goose.* Atlanta: Humanics Limited, 1989.

D'engenio, T. *Building With Tires.* Mass: Advisory for Open Ed., 1971.

D'engenio, T. *Building With Tubes.* Mass: Educ. Development Center, 1970.

Educational Facilities Lab. *Found Spaces and Equipment for Children's Centers.* New York: Educational Facilities Laboratory, 1972.

Galambos, J. *Play and Playgrounds.* NAEYC. Washington DC, 1974.

Kritchevsky and Prescott. *Planning Environments for Young Children.* NAEYC. Washington DC.

Miller, Peggy. *Creative Outdoor Play Areas.* New Jersey: Prentice Hall, Englewood Cliffs, 1972.

Sharkey, Tony. *Building a Playground.* Mass: Educational Development Center, 1970.

Warner and Guill. *Beautiful Junk.* U.S. Gov't. Printing Office, 1969.

Vergeront, J. *Places & Spaces for Pre-School and Primary (INDOORS).* NAEYC. Washington DC.

Facility Design for Early Childhood Programs Resource Guide #789 Washington DC, NAEYC.

Woodworking

Moffitt, H.M. *Woodworking for Children.* New York: ECEC Council of N.Y., 1968.

Pitcher, E. *Helping Young Children Learn.* 3rd ed. Ohio: Charles Merrill, 1979.

Skeen, P., Garner, A.P., and Cartwright, S. *Woodworking for Young Children.* NAEYC. Washington DC.

Block Building

Hirsch, L., ed. *Block Book.* NAEYC. Washington DC, 1984.

Johnson, H. *Art of Block Building.* New York: Bank Street College of Ed., 1966.

Starks, E. *Block Building.* Washington DC: EKNE, 1970.

Learning Activities

After reading some of the selected resources and seeing how your learning environments compare with what is listed in this guide, you can carry out some of the learning activities so as to be sure that your school environment is really planned to encourage all aspects of children's learning and development.

——1. Draw a plan of the classroom and identify how the present arrangement helps or hinders the children's use of materials, discipline, etc.

——2. Draw a plan of the outdoor or large muscle area and identify how the present arrangement helps or hinders the children's use of materials, group play, discipline, etc.

——3. Draw a plan for the indoor learning environment listing the centers of interest, the materials in each area, and state the reasons for the placement of the areas and for the use of the materials.

——4. Keep a record of children's use of equipment in the room indicating reactions to changes, identifying the possible need for changing some aspect of placement and storage of equipment, and indicating children's reactions to changes if any have been carried out.

——5. Repeat #4 in terms of outdoor environment.

Record observations of children using existing playground and identify problems and inadequacies, etc.

Draw up a plan of the existing outdoor learning environment and indicate planned changes, including reasons for the new plans.

When possible, keep a log of the changes, etc., planned and carried out where possible in the outdoor learning environment.

——6. Review classroom and playground arrangements to see how they encourage children to help themselves.

——7. Develop routines and schedules that help children make the best use of their learning environment, allow adequate time for children to develop their own activities, provide appropriate choices of activities for all children.

If you are working towards a Bilingual Specialization:

——8. Encourage children's use of both languages through materials, books, classroom signs and interactions with children.

Other Related Learning Resources and Activities
(Fill in your own resources.)

_____

_____

_____

_____

_____

_____

_____

_____

Competency Goal II

TO ADVANCE PHYSICAL AND INTELLECTUAL COMPETENCE

Functional Areas:
4. Physical
5. Cognitive
6. Communication
7. Creative

Children grow every minute of every day. Sometimes their growth is active and noisy, with the children pushing at the limits of what they know and do, and sometimes their lives are quiet; growth and development turns inward. But growth never stops, and some part of the child is always developing whether we are aware of it or not. We do not see the growth in the womb, but it is going on all the time for nine months. Once the baby is born, the silent push for growth is still present, but now we can see that the child is dependent on others to support many aspects of that growth.

We see the new teeth, measure the extra inches and pounds, but we don't see the changes in the mind. We can do a fairly effective job of supporting physical growth through nutrition, opportunities to exercise, health habits, etc. We are not nearly as sure that we are doing as effective or as good a job in helping children grow into thinking, feeling human beings. We do know children can't wait. Every day children grow and change. How they grow depends on their inheritance from their parents and even more on the world around them. If every minute is a growing minute, then it can't be repeated and must not be wasted.

There is a sequence and pattern to growth as well as an inner push. Just as growth is continuous and doesn't wait, periods of growth can't be repeated. A child can't waste the third year of his life in a poor environment with uncaring adults and then repeat it again. We can change, improve, and enrich this environment for the following year, but we don't know that, even if we do improve the environment, growth will be as complete as if the child had been well supported the year before.

Each part of children's development influences every other part as they begin to understand what their bodies can do. As their coordination and growth enable them to understand new things, they learn more about their world and develop an understanding of themselves.

Education must concern itself with helping children develop an inner mental structure so that they can organize all the information they acquire from their interaction with the environment. We do not always think of creativity as being an aspect of so-called individualized thinking, but it definitely is. If creativity implies finding new solutions to old problems, look-

19

ing at the world in different ways, and developing flexible attitudes of mind, then, as we allow children to explore different materials and try new experiences, we encourage not only their opportunities for seeing beauty in many unexpected places and expressing their own sensitive awareness to the world around them, but we are also helping them develop their abilities to think. Human beings learn by thinking about their actions. In fact, it is the connection between rational thought and action that makes human beings unique in the world.

As children develop the capabilities to think and create, they must also develop capabilities for sharing these ideas, feelings, and thoughts with others. The ability to use language to identify their increasing knowledge and sensory awareness helps them to further organize their growing understanding of themselves and their world. In order to understand and meet children's developmental needs, a teacher must know how children grow from year to year socially, emotionally, physically, and intellectually. The adult caring for young children should know what to expect of children from birth through age eight - what behavior is appropriate at any particular age, how to try to help children reach their fullest potential. Therefore, we should study child development as we begin to work in this competency.

The best way to really understand the children we work with, as well as the theoretical description of children's growth and development, is to *watch children !* Always remember that to know if you are effectively helping children learn, you must be aware of how they are reacting to what you do, and to what you say, to what you show them and give them to use. Observation can be general or designed to focus on particular aspects of growth - a child's small muscle coordination, his creativity, the behavior that indicates the quality of his or her self-concept, etc.

Resources

The following readings are suggested to help you as a teacher of young children learn about child development:

Biber, B. *Early Education and Psychological Development.* New Haven: Yale Univ. Press, 1984.

Engstrom, G., ed. *Play: The Child Strives Towards Self-Realization.* NAEYC. Washington DC.

Erikson, E. *Childhood and Society.* New York: Norton, 1950.

Helms and Turner. *Exploring Child Behavior.* Philadelphia: W.B. Saunders Co.

Katz, L. *What Should Young Children Be Doing:* The Wingspread Journal. Racine, Wisconsin: Johnson Foundation, 1987.

Gardner, D.B. *Development in Early Childhood.* New York: Harper & Row.

Salkind, N.J. and Ambron, S.R. *Child Development.* 5th ed. New York: Holt, Rinehart and Winston, 1987.

Stone, L.J. and Church, J. *Childhood and Adolescence.* 4th ed. New York: Random House, 1979.

Whordley, Derek, Ph.D. and Doster, Rebecca. *Humanics National Preschool Assessment Handbook - Users Guide for the Assessment Form for Ages 3-6.* Atlanta: Humanics Limited, 1983.

If we are truly supporting the physical and intellectual growth of children in a preschool program, we must have well-planned curriculum appropriate for preschool children. Below is a listing of readings to help you develop an overall awareness curriculum for young children. Select one or two readings and talk over your selection with your director, fellow teachers, early childhood specialist, or CDA advisor.

Abbott-Shim, Martha, Ph.D. and Sibley, Annette, Ph.D. *The Child Care Inventory.* Atlanta: Humanics Limited, 1986.

Bredekamp, D., ed. *Developmentally Appropriate Practice in Early Childhood Programs, Serving Children From Birth through Age 8.* NAEYC. Washington DC.

Coopersmith, S. and Feldman, R., ed. *The Formative Years Principles of Early Childhood Education.* California: Albione Publishing, 1974.

Langais, M. and Tipps, S. *Brain and Learning Directions in Early Childhood Education.* NAEYC. Washington DC, 1980.

Gordon, A.W. and Brown, K.W. *Beginnings and Beyond: Foundations in Early Childhood.* New York: Delman, 1985.

Montessori, M. *M. Montessori's Own Handbook.* 8th ed. New York: Schocken Books, 1914.

Pitcher, E. *Helping Young Children Learn.* 3rd ed. rev. Ohio: Charles Merrill, 1979.

Read, K., Gardner, B. and Mahler, C. *Early Childhood Programs Human Relationships and Learning.* 8th ed: Holt Rinehart and Winston, 1987.

Seefeldt, C., ed. *Early Childhood Curriculum - A Review of Current Research.* New York: Teachers College Press, Columbia Univ., 1986.

Seefeldt, C. and Barbour, N. *Early Childhood Education: An Introduction.* Columbus, Ohio: Merrill, 1986.

Spodeck, B., Saracho, O., and David, M.D. *Foundations of Early Childhood Education: Teaching Three-, Four- and Five-Year-Old Children.* New Jersey: Prentice-Hall, 1958.

Rudolph, M. *From Hand to Head.* New York: McGraw Hill, 1973.

Sponsellar, D. *"Play and Early Education",* B. Spodek, ed. *Handbook of Research in Early Childhood Education,* Lee Press.

Webber, E. *Ideas Influencing Early Childhood Education: A Theoretical Analysis.* New York: Teachers College Press. Columbia Univ. 1984.

Yardley, A. *Reaching Out, Exploration and Language, Discovering the Physical World, Senses and Sensitivity, The Teacher of Young Children, Young Children Thinking.* New York: Citation Press, Scholastic Magazine, 1973.

Learning Activities
The following learning activities are suggested as ways of providing teachers with a real understanding of young children's development and of the ways they learn.
——1. Keep regular anecdotal records, every day, on a child for three months and review them to observe patterns of behavior and aspects of growth.
——2. Complete some detailed evaluation form on three children in the class, covering social, emotional, physical, and intellectual development.

——3. Make a chart of children's development - intellectual, physical, social, and emotional - covering ages 0-5, using information gained from the readings. Such a chart can be used for staff development or parent education activities.

Other related learning resources and activities
(Fill in your own resources)

_____

_____

_____

_____

_____

_____

_____

_____

_____

_____

_____

_____

_____

_____

COMPETENCY GOAL II
FUNCTIONAL AREA 4 - PHYSICAL

Young children begin to know the world through their senses and the movements of their bodies. Their development involves the refining of muscle responses and the combining of specific and developed responses into total behavior. For example, children learn to use their arms and then their hands and fingers to hold things. Then they learn to hold a paint brush, use crayons, and write with a pencil. At the same time, they must learn to organize their knowledge and develop their coordination into the complex activities of drawing, reading, and writing. One of the first tasks for those of us who care for children is to provide an environment in which they can develop their physical skills. Growing children are active as their bodies change. They must have opportunities to use muscles and develop coordination, to practice and refine their muscular skills and coordination as they use their whole bodies to develop large muscle skills, and as they practice and refine their small motor skills by using their hands and eyes. They must develop and practice all the activities that enable them to coordinate both sensory input (i.e. what they hear, see, taste and smell) and muscular activity (what they do as it is based on what their senses tell them).

23

Functional Area 4

Physical Checklist *

A program that supports children's physical development must provide the space, equipment, and adult supervision to encourage children to use their bodies freely and with increasing skill and confidence. In order to encourage physical development, we should be aware of the following:

——1. Children have space to use their bodies in a variety of ways:
- ☐ To run, walk, climb, roll, jump, crawl, hop.
- ☐ To use wheel toys.
- ☐ To have an opportunity to develop these skills through games, dramatic play, and pantomime that help children make full use of their large muscles.

——2. Children are able to use different types of climbing, sliding, and balancing equipment at different levels of difficulty to permit them to have as wide a range of experience as possible in learning to use their large muscles.

——3. If possible there are a variety of environments in which children can move: formal playground, wooded areas, etc.

——4. Children have a variety of experiences using movement and rhythm through which they can learn to combine movement and auditory skills.

——5. Children have many opportunities for acting out and pantomiming a variety of ideas. Children should also have opportunities for unstructured movement.

——6. Children have many opportunities to explore concepts of space using their whole bodies (see Cognitive Development).

If you are working towards a Bilingual Specialization, you should be sure to use both languages in supporting all aspects of physical activities.

Resources
The following resources are suggested to help you plan and carry out programs that will support children's physical development.

Baker, K.R. *Let's Play Outdoors*. NAEYC. Washington DC.

Engstrom, G., ed. *The Significance of the Young Child's Motor Development*. NAEYC. Washington DC.

* This checklist may be copied for your portfolio.

Graham, Terry L., Ph.D. *Fingerplays and Rhymes for Always and Sometimes.* Atlanta: Humanics Limited, 1984.

Kamii, C. and DeVries, R. *Group Games in Early Education Implications of Piaget's Theory.* NAEYC. Washington DC.

Schrank, Rita. *Toddlers Learn By Doing.* Atlanta: Humanics Limited, 1985.

Seefeldt, C., ed. *Early Childhood Curriculum: A Review of Current Research.* Curtis, S. "New Views on Movement Development." New York: Teachers College Press, Columbia University, 1986.

Simpson, D. *Learning to Learn.* Ohio: Merrill, 1968.

Steen, Arleen, Ph.D. and Lane, Martha. *Teddy Bears at School.* Atlanta: Humanics Limited, 1986.

Sullivan, M. *Feeling Strong, Feeling Free; Movement Exploration for Young Children.* Washington DC.

Witkin, K. *To Move to Learn,* Pa. Temple Univ. Press, 1973

Learning Activities

The following activities are suggested as ways to help you support children's physical development.

——1. Plan, write down, and carry out in class a variety of sensory motor activities appropriate for the children and observe their reactions. Observe any change in children's behavior - increased motor skill and any other change that might be related to child's increased sensory motor skills.

——2. List activities to encourage large muscle development and coordination that can be carried out within the classroom. Write down a daily program and check to see if planning of activities allows for children to enjoy alternately quiet and active times during the day.

——3. Make a list of large muscle activities that do not require any use of equipment but depend on children's use of their bodies.

——4. List activities to encourage large muscle development and coordination that can be carried on outdoors.

——5. Observe children's use of indoor and outdoor play equipment that encourages large muscle development. Note children's specific reactions. Identify ways you can help them improve and refine their skills.

——6. List ways children can develop small muscle skills. Note which ones are already in use in the class. Plan and carry out new ones and record children's reactions.

If you are working towards a Bilingual Specialization:

——7. Identify games, chants, and songs in both languages to support children's play.

Other Related Learning Resources and Activities
(Fill in your own resources.)

_____

_____

_____

_____

_____

_____

_____

_____

_____

_____

_____

_____

_____

_____

_____

_____

COMPETENCY GOAL II
FUNCTIONAL AREA 5 - COGNITIVE

As we have noted before, children's education consists of their developing a framework of thinking into which they can organize their growing body of knowledge about their world. Our job as teachers is to help them develop these organizational skills, to increase their awareness of as many different aspects of their environment as we can, without confusing them. We must remember always that children's knowledge of their world begins in their knowledge of themselves, and we must present new information to them in ways to which they can relate directly. They must taste, feel, see, smell and hear for themselves. In order to support and stimulate children's cognitive development, we, as teachers of young children, must provide them not only with a well-organized learning environment, but also the materials, equipment, and supportive interactions of adults.

27

Functional Area 5
Cognitive Checklist *

We must develop an understanding of the learning process and plan carefully to support children's learning by working in the following ways:

——1. We plan, organize, and use materials, activities, and experiences to encourage children to explore, satisfy curiosity, and gain firsthand experiences in their world.

- [ ] New themes or concepts are introduced with experiences that relate directly to the children themselves.
- [ ] Children are given opportunities to use all their senses.
- [ ] The classroom is orderly and materials are easy to reach, encouraging children to touch and try.
- [ ] Unstructured materials including paint, clay, crayons, paper, scissors, water, sand, blocks, are provided regularly for children to use during the free-choice activity period.
- [ ] The centers of interest are well-equipped and materials are changed and added to meet children's changing interests.
- [ ] Children's need to touch, smell, taste, and hear is accepted and encouraged - unsafe materials are not within reach.
- [ ] Children are offered many types of experiences to explain different concepts or teach different skills; for example, they can pour water, sand, paint, and milk into many different kinds of containers to understand full and empty and to learn to pour using small muscles and eye-hand coordination.

——2. We are aware that children have not had much experience and often reach incorrect, though logical, conclusions. For example, children say:

"If I eat and sleep here, I live here now and I won't go home."

"If Mom goes away, how do I know I'll see her again?"

"If the bus leaves now, how do I go home again?"

"If Mommy is not there, no one will take care of me."

"If being dirty is bad and I spill something, I'm bad."

We help children to understand how things really are.

---

*This checklist may be copied for your portfolio.

——3. We encourage children to experience, question, and find answers and solutions to real problems. Encourage them to identify casual relationships in what they see, do, and experience. The work necessary to running the class is organized so children can perform real chores in acceptable ways.

☐ Children take part in real experiences - shopping, cooking, shoveling snow, clean up, etc.

☐ Children are helped to make contact with the real world - exploring their school and then the local community, visiting stores, firehouse, library, boat yards, bakeries, etc.

☐ Visits to farms, zoos, greenhouses, gardens, are arranged.

☐ Children meet the people who keep things functioning in their immediate environment:

☐ Teachers, by their behavior, model respect for all workers and verbally define their jobs.

☐ Community people are invited into class. Teachers make visitors aware of children's capacities to understand and visits are followed with books, stories, pictures, etc., relating to the work done by visitors.

——4. In carefully planned ways, we help children become aware of how they receive information about the world through their visual, tactile and auditory senses; children are thus helped to use their senses as a way of examining their environment.

——5. There is a variety of construction materials regularly available - blocks, collage materials, wood for woodwork and glue structures, construction toys, etc.

——6. There is a variety of selected science materials and activities and specific pieces of equipment (electricity, magnets, prisms, etc.) for children to use so they can experiment and discover. Sizes and shapes of containers for water and sand are selected so children can experiment with quantity, shape, size, volume, full, empty, etc.

——7. Children's understanding of spatial relationships is encouraged by:

☐ Using manipulative toys that fit together and come apart.

☐ Learning about where things are in school and home, becoming aware of and verbalizing about direction of movement to/from, in/out, etc.

☐ Having chances to rearrange items in space - folding, stacking, twisting.

☐ Having chances to view the world from different spatial points of view - hanging from jungle gym, etc.

☐ Having chances to learn about positional relationships - by moving about in the classroom; in the middle, at the side, on/off, through, apart, together; etc.

——8. Experiences with concepts of number and quantity are provided through:

☐ Opportunities to quantify and to establish one-to-one correspondence, setting tables, etc. Counting concrete objects (cookies, etc.).

☐ Identifying number names with quantities.

Serving food, a little, a lot, many/few, etc.

——9. Experiences with temporal relationships are provided by:

☐ Patterning activities to demonstrate ideas of sequence.

☐ Using and talking about sequence - first, last; now, later, etc.

☐ Moving with different and changing rates of movement - fast, slow, etc.

☐ Using the vocabulary of time - morning, afternoon, today, tomorrow, week, etc.

☐ Using clocks and calendars as part of the regular school routine and helping children understand what they are used for.

☐ Comparing time periods - short, long; old, new, etc.

☐ Describing past events and future events by talking, planning, etc. i.e. birthdays and holidays.

——10. Children's understanding of categorization is encouraged by:

☐ Helping children learn to sort by size, shape, and color.

☐ Helping children learn to sort by usage.

☐ Helping children learn to sort by sensory perception.

☐ Helping children make comparisons of similarities and differences.

☐ Helping children learn that things can be sorted in different ways by more than one attribute.

☐ Helping children learn by positive and negative statements.

——11. Children's understanding of ideas of seriation is developed by:

☐ Helping children learn to make comparisons by size, weight, texture, loudness, and color.

☐ Helping children learn to arrange items in order by different dimensions, size, and length.

☐ Helping children learn to make quantitative comparisons - more, less, same.

☐ Helping children to compare quantity by matching in one-to-one correspondence.

——12. Ideas of change are developed through cooking, working with seeds, raising animals, and observing and recording children's own growth.

——13. We provide for learning and development to proceed from simple to increasingly complex levels, by the choice of materials, experiences and activities.

——14. Children are helped to go from simple exploration to imitative play, complex play, to talking about play, describing play, and verbalizing about plans for play by providing support through time, materials, and adult acceptance.

——15.The use of symbols to designate words and numbers is a developmental process - part of children's developing an understanding of levels of representation. This use of symbols is encouraged by:

☐ Exposing children to symbols and understanding that their interest indicates readiness to work with symbols.

☐ Providing children with opportunities to use letters, numbers, etc. No one is forced to participate in such activities if they are not interested and ready.

——16. We play alongside children in a non-directive manner when children seem to need models to stimulate their usage of materials and equipment. For example, "I am going to pile these blocks here," "May I visit in your house?", etc.

——17. We provide some representational activity after each experience varying with the age of the children, including opportunities to use art media, retelling experiences and using photographs, reading stories, and using dramatic play materials. (Children are not required to reproduce what they have experienced at any given time.)

——18. We offer learning experiences in unstructured and then structured ways:

☐ Teachers specifically explain certain concepts after children have had a chance to explore materials in their own way. They provide structured materials and time for each child to use each day, offering materials in ways that focus children's attention on what they are doing, and build their understanding of increasingly complex concepts.

If you are working towards a Bilingual Specialization, you need to use the language most familiar to each child to provide learning experiences that lead to understanding of basic concepts.*

Resources

Since the bibliography is so extensive, it has been broken down into subject related areas; such as science, math, etc. This bibliography covers the cognitive and physical functional areas. Talk to fellow teachers, early childhood specialists and choose a few readings in each area.

Cognitive

Biber, B., Shapiro, E. and Wickens, D. *Promoting Cognitive Growth - A Developmental Interaction Point of View.* 2nd ed. NAEYC. Washington DC.

Brown, J.F., ed. *Curriculum Planning for Young Children.* NAEYC. Washington DC.

Castle, Kathryn, Ph.D. *The Infant & Toddler Handbook.* Atlanta: Humanics Limited, 1983.

Christman-Rothlein, Liz, Ph.D. and Caballero, Jane Ph.D. *Back to Basics in Early Reading Skills.* Atlanta: Humanics Limited, 1981.

Commins, Elaine, Ph.D. *Early Childhood Activities.* Atlanta: Humanics Limited, 1982.

Forman, G. and Kuscher, D. *The Child's Construction of Knowledge: Piaget for Teaching Children.* NAEYC. Washington DC.

Frank, L. *Play Is Valid.* Washington DC: ACEI, 1968.

Gordon, I. *Baby Learning Through Baby Play.* New York: St. Martins Press, 1970.

Gordon, I. *Child Learning Through Child Play.* New York: St. Martins Press, 1972.

Hohmann, M., Banet, B. and Weikart, D. *Young Children in Action.* Yslanti, Michigan: The High Scope Press, 1979.

Labinowicz, E. *The Paper Primer.* Mass: Addison-Wesley, 1980.

Landreth, C. *Preschool Teaching and Learning.* New York: Harper & Row, 1972.

Lerner, J. Mardell-Czudnowski and Goldenberg, D. *Special Education for the Early Childhood Years.* New Jersey: Prentice Hall, 1987.

Lorton, M. *Workjobs.* Reading, Mass: Addison-Wesley, 1975.

Moffit, M. *Intellectual Content of Play.* ECEC of New York.

Montessori, M. *M. Montessori's Own Handbook.* New York: Schocken Books, 1965.

Paley, V. *Mollie is Three: Growing Up in School.* Chicago: University of Chicago Press, 1986.

Rudolph, M. *From Hand to Head.* New York: McGraw-Hill, 1973.

Sharp, E. *Thinking Is Child's Play.* New York: Discuss Books, 1969.

Rogers, C.S. and Sawyers, J. *Play in the Lives of Children.* NAEYC. Washington DC.

*CDA competency standards and Assessment system. CDA National Credentialing Program, Washington DC.

Schickendanz, F. *More Than the ABC's: The early stages of reading and writing.* NAEYC. Washington DC.

Trencher, Barbara. *Child's Play.* Atlanta: Humanics Limited, 1976.

Warner and Gwill. *Beautiful Junk.* DHEW. OCD Washington DC. OCD Publication #73-1036

Mathematics

Baratta-Lorton, M. *Mathematics Their Way.* Menlo Park: Addison-Wesley, 1976.

Caballero, Jane, Ph.D. *Month-by-Month Activity Guide.* Atlanta: Humanics Limited, 1981.

Kamii, C. *Number in Preschool and Kindergarten* Educational Implications of Piaget's Theory. NAEYC. Washington DC.

Peterson, R.and Felton-Collins, V. *The Piaget Handbook For Teachers and Parents.* New York: Teachers College Press, Columbia University, 1986.

Sharp, E. *Thinking is Child's Play.* New York: Discuss Books, Avon Publishing, 1969.

Steen, Arleen, Ph.D. and Lane, Martha L. *Teddy Bears at School.* Atlanta: Humanics Limited, 1986.

Science

Bruno, J. and P. Dalian. *Cooking in the Classroom.* California: Fearon Publishers.

Caballero, Jane, Ph.D. *Aerospace Projects for Young Children.* Atlanta: Humanics Limited, 1987.

Caballero, Jane, Ph.D. *Aviation & Space Education - Folder Games.* Atlanta: Humanics Limited, 1986.

Carmichael, V. *Science Experiences for Young Children.* SCAEYC. California: 1974.

Croft, K.B. *Good for Me Cookbook.* NYU Leadership Development Program, Project Head Start.

Diener, Carolyn, et al. *Energy - Curriculum for 3-,4- and 5-Year-olds.* Atlanta: Humanics Limited, 1981.

Goodwin, M. and Pollen, S. *Creative Food Experiences for Children.* rev. Washington DC: Center for Science in the Public Interest, 1980.

Griffith, L. *Big Questions and Little Children, Science & Head Start.* HEW-OCD.

Hawkins, D. *Messing About in Science, Occasional Paper.* Mass: Early Childhood Education Study, Educ. Devel. Center, 1969.

Hill, Dorothy M. *Mud, Sand, and Water.* NAEYC. Washington DC, 1974.

Holt, B. *Science with Young Children.* NAEYC. Washington DC.

Knight, Michael, Ph.D. and Graham, Terry, Ph.D. *The Leaves Are Falling In Rainbows -. Science Activities.* Atlanta: Humanics Limited, 1984.

Pitcher, E. *Helping Young Children Learn.* 3rd ed. Ohio: Charles Merrill, 1979.

Throop, S. *Science for the Young Child.* California: Fearon Pub., 1974.

Williams, R., Rockwell, R. and Sherwood, E. *Mudpies to Magnets: A Preschool Science Curriculum.* Minnesota: Toys 'n' Things Press, 1987.

Yardley, Alice. *Discovering the Physical World.* New York: Citation Press, 1973.

Block Building

Hirsch, L., ed. *The Block Book.* NAEYC. Washington DC.

Johnson, H. *Art of Block Building.* New York: Bank Street College of Education, 1966.

Starks, E. *Blockbuilding.* New York: EKNE, 1970.

Stewart, A. "Magic of Blocks." *Instructor.* November, 1973.

Woodworking

Moffitt, M. *Woodworking for Children.* ECEC. New York, 1968.

Skeen, P., Garner, A.P. and Cartwright, S. *Woodworking for Young Children.* NAEYC. Washington DC.

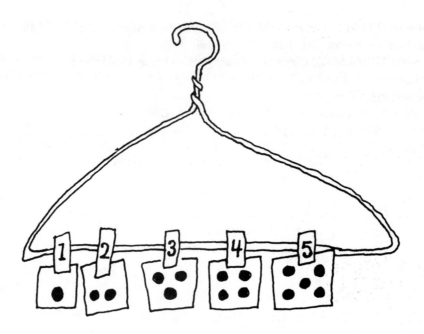

Learning Activities

The following learning activities will help us strengthen and improve all these areas of the curriculum.

A. Physical and Cognitive Development

——1. Write a case study on a child describing his physical, social, emotional, intellectual, and language development giving examples of his behavior. Offer your suggestions and recommendations for furthering his development.

Discuss this child with your director. Describe any actions taken and if outside specialist help has been/is being sought.

B. Cognitive

——1. Identify basic shapes and ways of teaching children shape discrimination. find at least eight ways to make children aware of shapes in all learning areas of the room.

——2. Identify concepts of number seriation to be taught to preschool children. Design or identify games and materials to help children understand one-to-one correspondence during their everyday lives.

——3. Design and make learning games to teach specific concepts - describe game, make note of concepts to be taught by the game, and note children's reactions.

——4. Keep anecdotal records weekly on the children in the class with an emphasis on identifying intellectual growth in individual children. (see page 78)

——5. List eight ways of helping children learn about their awareness of themselves in space during daily classroom activities.

——6. Keep written lesson plans on a regular basis, identifying daily programs and special learning activities. Keep daily records of any changes in the daily routines and activities and list reasons for the changes.

C. Block Buildings

——1. Using the information in the readings, set up a well-organized block area, marking the shape of the blocks on the shelves and identifying and adding the necessary block accessory equipment.

——2. Observe and record children's reactions to the organization of the materials in the block area. Observe and record their behavior during cleanup and free play periods

——3. Plan, carry out, and record specific activities planned to encourage and stimulate block building in the class, such as introducing different block accessory materials. Keep a record of children's reactions.

D. Science

——1. Set up a science area in the classroom using the information from the readings and the checklist to decide what to include, where to place the area, and how to set out and store materials.

——2. Using information from the readings, identify areas of scientific investigation - themes - appropriate to the preschool age level and identify activities that will help children gain information and develop concepts in each of these areas.

——3. Plan and carry out a series of science activities to use with children in the class. Group the activities about specific themes - use of senses, concept of change, how things work, what plants and animals need to live, nature of air temperature, etc. Do the same for outdoor science activities.

Keep a record of the children's reactions. Do they begin to make comparisons about activities on their own, remember other activities, etc? How interested are they?

Based on your readings, describe the reasons for each of the activities used with the children. List the children's books used with each activity.

——4. Identify a bibliography of books relating to science in the preschool curriculum. Make a file of this science bibliography with a file card for each book listing:

- ☐ 1. Subject area
- ☐ 2. Book title
- ☐ 3. Author(s)
- ☐ 4. Illustrator and publisher
- ☐ 5. Summary of book
- ☐ 6. Activities motivated by book
- ☐ 7. Cross reference if any

——5. Plan and carry out a field trip (can be outdoors or within the school building) related to one science theme that gives children opportunity to observe, name, collect and classify objects.

—6. Observe in another classroom. Identify all activities related to science learning (displays, materials, books, collections, field trips). Identify and describe the role of the teacher in helping children to raise questions, search for answers, experiment, and clarify understandings of basic concepts.

If you are working towards a Bilingual Specialization:
—7. Identify learning materials and bibliographies of children's books in their first language.
—8. Encourage children to use materials and express their understanding of basic concepts in their first language and in English.

Other related learning resources and activities
(Fill in your own resources)

_____

_____

_____

_____

_____

_____

_____

_____

_____

_____

_____

_____

_____

COMPETENCY II
FUNCTIONAL AREA 6 - COMMUNICATION

The ability to share ideas through words sets human beings apart from all other members of the animal kingdom.

From the beginning of life, children hear sounds of many kinds. They become aware that the sounds they produce - crying at first - cause certain reactions. They learn to identify the voices of those who care for them and then to distinguish specific sounds. They gradually become aware that the sounds they hear have specific meaning. As they hear different sounds, they try to copy them and gradually develop the ability to coordinate tongue, lips, and facial muscles so they can produce different sounds at will. They learn to reproduce the sounds that are part of the language of those who care for them. Babies and very young children love to be talked and sung to and to have the sounds they make repeated back to them. As they grow into their second year, they "absorb" language from their environment as those who care for them put words to the objects around them and to their actions. As the adults who care for children really listen to them, children are encouraged to talk and to share their own ideas. In an interesting and accepting world where the adults who care for them understand the importance of talking to and listening to children, language and the ability and desire to communicate can develop quite rapidly.

By the time children come into preschool programs or play groups of one kind or another, we hope that they have learned to communicate needs and feelings, and to identify, by words, different aspects of their environment, such as objects and experiences.

In a preschool program, we should be concerned with helping children develop vocabulary, improve their ability to express themselves, and describe their experiences and feelings. At the same time, by listening to and accepting what children have to say, we help them develop the ability to listen to other children and adults. By exchanging ideas and observations, children are developing the social aspect of their communication skills. As children develop their understanding of how spoken words refer to aspects of their experiences, their parents and teachers should also be helping them understand how pictures and words are also ways of representing their feelings, ideas and experiences. We should provide pictures that relate directly to what children know - simple picture books for toddlers, then short, easily understood illustrated stories that describe familiar places, people, and activities. Children begin to understand and enjoy accounts of feelings and experiences similar to their own. At the same time, teachers and parents can begin to help children put their speech into written words by writing down what children describe and report about their experiences and their picture representation of their ideas. In this way, we are helping children to develop into thinking, communicating human beings.

In order to support this process, those of us teaching in preschool programs must organize, plan, and enrich children's environment in every way. We must provide things to do and think about, pictures to look at, people to read to them, and most of all, grownups who care about them and are interested in listening and talking to them.

As we care for infants and children by holding them and caring for physical needs, we communicate to them our feelings by our actions. We give children a sense of security, of being able to trust their world to be a safe place in which to grow, explore, and develop. As we care for children in a school setting, we demonstrate our acceptance, concern, and affection by the way we treat children, how we listen to them, by the kind of environment we provide, both physical and emotional. Thus children are sharing, by our example and their own inter-actions, effective and positive non-verbal ways of communicating. To help children develop communication skills, these processes must take place for all children and this means we must work with children in whatever language their first communication experiences take place.

Schools for young children must, therefore, be prepared to provide language experiences in languages other than English when necessary.

We went on the bus
to the park.
I went on the swings.
David and I fed the ducks.
We found a leaf and a rock.
When we got back to school
we put them on the table.

Functional Area 6

Communication Checklist*

As teachers of young children, we must provide an environment in which children feel free to develop all their skills in interpersonal communications:

——1. We are accepting of the children with whom we work by:

☐ Encouraging and accepting all children's communications, verbal and non-verbal.

☐ Avoiding all occasions for ridicule or downgrading of children's activities or speech.

☐ Accepting children's need to be silent or withdrawn on occasion.

☐ Really listening to children, getting down to their level or picking them up if needed and taking time so children can talk at their own pace.

☐ Providing a good speaking model with a pleasant voice.

☐ Indicating acceptance of any form of children's speech, although we model the language in common use as we talk to them.

☐ Having children show us what they need and keeping non-verbal contact as this is done, when we can't understand them or are not sure of what they mean.

——2. We demonstrate that we really listen to children to understand their meanings by:

☐ Showing them we are aware of what is happening at home by listening with understanding to each child.

☐ Responding to what a child tells us; "You saw a big truck; was it red?"

☐ Listening to one child carefully without rejecting another's need for attention. We establish a physical contact (hold a hand, etc.) with another child as we listen to the first.

☐ Helping children talk about their feelings and concerns. For example: "Your finger really hurts,""Mommy/Daddy will meet you when you come home,""You're really angry with John,""That hurts Mary when you hit her."

——3. We interact with children and maintain an environment which will provide them with opportunities to develop and broaden their vocabulary, their expressive and receptive skills, and their ability to develop understanding through the various levels of representation. We:

☐ Observe and comment consistently on what is happening during the school day - weather, food, trips, bus rides, etc.

☐ Comment on all aspects of change in daily life - weather, plant, animal, child growth, and cooking.

*This checklist may be copied for your portfolio

☐ .Question the results of children's exploration and experimentation where children don't usually verbalize their activities.

☐ Verbally label materials, activities, and experiences regularly for children.

☐ Clarify children's verbal observations when necessary. For example: Child, "I like them;" Teacher, "You like those red shoes."

——4. We use a wide variety of techniques to encourage speech. We:

☐ Read and tell stories to children.

☐ Sing songs to and with children.

☐ Use tape recorder to record, experiment, tell stories to listen to, and tell stories requiring answers.

☐ Encourage children to retell stories they know.

☐ Encourage children to participate in choral speaking.

☐ Encourage children to make up their own words to songs and stories, initiating this by the use of folk songs, nursery rhymes.

☐ Encourage children to converse among themselves at snack, group time, and during play activities by providing opportunities for children to be together in small groups of two and three.

☐ Encourage children to make up stories and poems of their own.

——5. We encourage progressively more complex sentence structure by:

☐ Starting with simple verbal labeling.

☐ Using an increasing variety of words.

☐ Providing models of increasing complex sentence structure.

☐ Helping children talk about their activities, what they are doing or have accomplished.

——6. To help children develop their understanding of written forms of communication, we provide children with opportunities to recognize symbols for words and numbers by providing them with the opportunities to develop understanding through the various levels of representation.* In our classrooms, and as part of our curriculum we:

☐ Provide opportunities for children to recognize objects by different cues - sound, touch, and smell, help children recognize objects.

☐ Provide opportunities for children to play out life situations - socio-dynamic play - enacting social roles using language, actions, and objects to represent real situations: dramatic play in doll corner, dramatic play in block area, and dramatic play outdoors.

☐ Provide opportunities for children to imitate specific actions, i.e. "This is how we brush our teeth," etc.

☐ Provide opportunities for children to make simple representational models using blocks, cardboard boxes, and unstructured materials and to identify their representations verbally if they are ready and willing to do so.

*Weikart, D., *The Cognitively Oriented Curriculum.* NAEYC. Washington DC

——7. We arrange for all activities, materials, etc., to be represented pictorially so children learn that pictures stand for real objects; objects are matched to pictures and pictures to objects, including:

☐ Pictures of socio-dramatic activities - men and women building, working, cooking, etc.

☐ Labels for toys, materials, and equipment with appropriate, pictures for storage, etc.

☐ Providing stories and written descriptions that relate to children's own experiences.

☐ .Very simple experience charts for cooking experiences using pictures and words.

☐ Pictures and books relating to specific items at the same science table.

☐ Providing name cards for children with a sign to help them recognize their names - each child has his/her name and sign on cubbies, cots, etc.

——8. If you are working towards a Bilingual Specialization and desire to help the children whose primary language is not English, we should provide language experience and support for the development of communication skills in the children's own language as effectively as possible. If we are not bilingual, we still demonstrate acceptance of the children by including their own language when we can in the group setting, and helping them use it as a bridge to another language for the sake of increased communication. We can work with bilingual children by:

☐ Accepting and using children's primary language when possible, using common expressions, and using joint bilingual labeling of materials.

☐ Using or arranging for a helper or interpreter to use children's primary language to communicate necessities as children start the program and to introduce new ideas and concepts.

☐ Using songs, stories, and possibly games, using both languages.

Resources

The following bibliography contains information to help us understand language development in young children and to work effectively with curriculum for supporting language and communication skills.

Casden, C. *Language in Early Childhood Education.* rev. NAEYC, 1981.

Hodges and Rudolph. *Language and Learning to Read.* New York: Houghton Mifflin, 1972.

Hohlmann, M., Banet, B. and Weikart, D. *Young Children in Action, A Manual for Preschool Education.* Michigan: The High Scope Press, 1979.

Jett-Simpson, Mary, Ph.D. *Reading Resource Book - Parents and Beginning Reading.* Atlanta: Humanics Limited, 1986.

Mann, Lynne. *The EARLI Program - Receptive/Expressive Language Development.* Vol. I and II. Atlanta: Humanics Limited, 1982.

Pitcher, E. *Helping Young Children Learn.* 3rd ed. rev. Ohio: Charles Merrill, 1979.

Read, K. *The Nursery School.* 6th ed. Philadelphia: W.B. Saunders, 1976.

Schickendanz, J. *More Than ABC's.* NAEYC. Washington DC, 1986.

Seefeldt, C. *Early Childhood Curriculum, A review of Current Research.* New York: Teachers College Press, Columbia Univ. 1986.

Yardley, A. *Exploration and Language.* Young Children's Learning Series, Citation Press, New York, 1973.

Bicultural/Bilingual Education*

Bernbaum, M. *Early Childhood Programs for Non-English Speaking Children.* Albany, New York:State Univ. of N.Y., State Educ. Dept., Division of General Education.

Escobedo,T. *Early Childhood Bilingual Education - A Hispanic Perspective.* New York: Teachers College Press, Columbia Univ., 1983.

Hale-Benson, J. *Black Children: Their roots, culture and learning styles.* rev. Baltimore: Johns Hopkins Univ. Press, 1986.

Montoya, J. "A Case for Bilingualism" *Instructor.* February, 1975.

A Better Chance to Learn:Bilingual, Bicultural Education, U.S. Commission on Civil Rights, Clearing House Publications 51, Washington DC, 1975.

Ramsey, P. *Teaching and Learning in a Diverse World - Multicultural Education for Young Children.* New York: Teachers College Press, Columbia Univ., 1987.

Saracho, O.N. and Spodek, B., ed. *Understanding the Multicultural Experience in Early Childhood Education.* NAEYC. Washington DC, 1983.

Williams, L.R. and DeGaetano, Y. *ALERTA A multicultural, bilingual approach to teaching young children.* Reading, Mass: Addison-Wesley, 1985.

Following is a list of books related to using literature with young children. We can use carefully chosen stories and poems to help children develop an understanding of the world around them, their experiences and feelings, and help them realize relationships between speech, ideas, and reading.

Burke, E.M. *Early Childhood Literature: For Love of child and Book.* Boston: Allyn and Bacon, 1986.

Commins, Elaine. *Lessons from Mother Goose.* Atlanta: Humanics Limited, 1989.

Jacobs, L. *Using Literature with Young Children.* New York: Teachers College Press, Columbia Univ., 1965.

Oppenheim, J., Brenner, B., and Boegehold, B. *Choosing Books for Kids.* New York: Ballantine Books, 1987.

Sutherland, Z. *The Best in Children's Books - The University of Chicago's Guide to Children's Literature, 1979-1984.* Chicago: Univ. of Chicago Press, 1986.

Trelease, J. *The Read-Aloud Handbook.* New York: Penguin, 1982.

Wendelin, Karla, Ph.D. and Greenlaw, Jean, Ph.D. *Storybook Classrooms - Using Children's Literature in the Learning Center.* Atlanta: Humanics Limited, 1984.

Learning Activities - Enhancing Communication

As we work out some of the following activities with children, we will be improving our competencies in helping children enhance language and communication skills.

—1. Keep a log for a week, noting the verbal interactions between self and a particular child.

*See also bibliography relating to child's sense of self.

——2. Keep a log for a week, noting specific activities that lead to verbal interaction between the children.

——3. Using information in the readings and from experience, identify and describe activities that can be used to enhance language development and stimulate verbal interaction.

——4. Examine one or two reading readiness programs and choose appropriate activities that can be used in preschool.

——5. Identify and list teacher behavior that encourages or inhibits verbal interaction and use of language skills.

——6. Observe in another classroom and identify and describe three language arts activities. Describe the activities, materials needed, and children's and teacher's behavior.

——7. Using cooking activities as a focus, plan a series of language activities for children which encourages their verbal participation. Prepare experience charts that can be utilized for teaching recognition of symbols, stimulating recall and ability to follow instructions, and developing new vocabulary.

——8. Make a tape recording of one communication experience (storytelling and discussion, listening game, choral speaking, etc.). Listen to it with children, encouraging their reactions and comments.

——9. Design materials that will help children broaden vocabulary and improve expressive skills. Identify reasons for using the materials, describe materials used and ways to make the materials.

——10. Assemble ideas and materials for parents to use to help children develop language skills and reading readiness skills.

The following are learning activities to help us develop competency in using literature with young children.

——1. Identify 75 books for use in the preschool program relating to areas of interest in the classroom and relating to children's developmental needs, their feelings, ethnic backgrounds, real experiences at home and at school and then:

Make a file card on each book listing:

☐ 1. Subject area (functional area)
☐ 2. Book title
☐ 3. Author(s)
☐ 4. Illustrator and publisher
☐ 5. Summary of book
☐ 6. Activities motivated by book
☐ 7. Cross reference

——2. Read selected stories to individual children and to small groups and note children's reactions. These reactions can be noted on cards and included in the book file.

——3. Introduce poetry to the classroom. Keep a list of the poetry you have used and of the children's reactions.

——4. Identify and describe reasons for using appropriate literature with young children to demonstrate your own understanding of the use of literature in preschool programs.

If you are working towards a Bilingual Specialization, the following activities will relate to bilingual enrichment for children whose primary language is not English.

——1. Prepare a list of everyday expressions, teacher instructions, and basic items used in the classroom, and arrange for the list to be translated by a parent and posted in the classroom. Utilize the words in the classroom as you and your fellow teachers learn them.

——2. Invite a bilingual/bicultural parent to the class to tell stories and teach songs to the children. Describe the children's reactions.

——3. Invite a bilingual/bicultural parent to the class to carry out specific classroom activities with the teacher such as cooking.

——4. Design a play activity or game utilizing non-English words.

——5. Investigate bilingual resources, people, places, and learning materials available in your area to teachers of young children.

Other Related Learning Resources and Activities
(Fill in your own resources.)

_____

_____

_____

_____

_____

_____

_____

_____

_____

_____

_____

_____

_____

COMPETENCY GOAL II
FUNCTIONAL AREA 7 - CREATIVE

The human capacity to think creatively appears in children's earliest experiences with their environment. Their world is brand new to them, and they are constantly receiving new sensations. As they begin to reach out towards their environment, they become aware that they can affect the world around them - they touch a mobile, and it moves; they bang a toy, and it jingles. Adults around them respond to these first outward actions and either encourage new and different responses or begin to place limits on children's attempts to actively relate to their world. By the time children come into a preschool program, they have developed patterns of reacting to the environment of people and things. Hopefully they will be ready to try and develop relationships with new people, to try to use new materials and equipment. Then when they have explored and experimented with this new environment and feel secure, they will try to find new ways of playing with other children, creating new roles, and using equipment and materials in different ways. This practice of looking at their world through different views, of exploring and experimenting may well be the best preparation we can give them to deal with the world they will face as adults.

Our world is changing so rapidly that, apart from the fact that it will change, we can predict little else about it. The changes will create new situations and problems and these will require new and creative solutions. We must, therefore, help our children discover new ways of using old things, and new ways of thinking about themselves and their capacities. They must be helped to develop confidence to try, experiment and explore.

45

Functional Area 7

Creative Checklist *

Creativity is far more than the ability to paint a picture or make up a new tune. Our responsibility as teachers of young children is to create a physical and emotional environment in which children can develop confidence in the value of their own ideas. Concern and interest in each child and acceptance of their ideas and explorations give children the courage to try new paths - this attitude of acceptance and support for children's creative investigation of their environment is important to children's development in this area. If they feel accepted and supported, they will think about and use all aspects of their environment in creative ways.

There are many ways in which we as teachers of young children can provide an environment which encourages and challenges them to explore, experiment, and interact creatively with people and things.

——1. We plan for and support children's exploration by:

☐ Arranging for children to have the opportunity to use unstructured materials in the room - sand, water, clay, paint, and large blocks. There is no right or wrong way, only their way.

☐ Planning for equipment outdoors that will allow children to rearrange their environment - large, light blocks, tubes to crawl in, earth to dig and move, and areas for planting.

——2. We plan for and support children's expressive activities in the area of art by providing:

☐ A variety of creative art media in a well-planned art center (see Functional Area 3) such as clay, play dough, paint, sand, crayons, and collage materials.

☐ Many opportunities for children to become fully aware of each art medium and their own feelings about them.

☐ Many opportunities for children to satisfy their initial interest in the process, not the product, by experimenting with art materials with no pressure to produce a product.

——3. We encourage dramatic play activities by supporting and developing the play impulses in symbolic and dramatic form. A well planned and organized play center is set up offering children a variety of structured and unstructured materials that encourage imaginative dramatic play (see Functional Area 3). We should also:

☐ Model dramatic play activities - come to tea parties, etc.

☐ Know when to initiate dramatic play activity and when to withdraw once children are involved.

*This checklist may be copied for your portfolio.

☐ Provide a repertoire of dramatic play responses through storytelling, use of puppets (all teachers should be able to act), and acting out stories, etc.

——4. We provide a variety of experiences with sound through the use of voice, and homemade and standard musical instruments. Children are encouraged to sing, make up their own words to folk songs, and compose poetry and tunes, independently and with teacher support.

——5. We encourage exploration and experimentation by:

☐ Providing children with the means to explore their physical environment through science activities, such as water, sand, magnetism, earth, etc.

☐ Providing new additions to existing materials and equipment that encourage children to use the materials in new combinations, new ways.

——6. We can provide and maintain an emotionally accepting environment in which children feel free to try, explore, experiment, and "create." We do this by:

☐ *Never* drawing pictures for children because it sets unreasonable standards for them.

☐ Always suggesting children do things themselves and providing only the support of adult presence, affection and acceptance.

☐ Giving opportunities for children to use all art media on an experimental basis with no pressure for any product.

☐ Letting children choose if they want to store or hang up products, never imposing adult standards of what to keep and what to throw away.

☐ Recognizing children's interest and involvement with materials regardless of the results; saying for example, "You really worked hard."

☐ Providing storage at school if home is not accepting of child's efforts, and trying to help parents understand school's goals in this area.

☐ Allowing children time to explore, manipulate, and experiment without a sense of rush or without having to cut such experiences short unnecessarily.

If you are working towards a Bilingual Specialization, you should:

——7. Support children's creative activities in their first language.

——8. Bring the art, music, and dance from children's own culture into the classroom.

Resources

The following resources contain ideas and information that should be helpful in establishing and maintaining the physical and emotional environment that will support and encourage children's creative interactions with their world.

Biber, B. *Children's Drawings,* N.Y., Bank Street College of Education, 1962.

Caplan, F. *Power of Play,* N.Y., Doubleday, Anchor Press, 1974.

Cass, J. *Helping Children Grow Through Play,* N.Y., Schocken Books, 1973.

Cherry, R. *Creative Movements for the Developing Child.* California: Fearon Pub., 1974.

Engstrom, G., ed. *Play: the Child Strives Toward Self-Realization.* NAEYC. Washington DC.

Feing, E., Rivkin, M. eds. *The Young Child at Play - Reviews of Research Vol. 4.* NAEYC. Washington DC.

Frank, L. "Play is Valid," *Childhood Education.* NAEYC. March, 1968. PP.433-440

Frank, L. "Play, The Essential Ingredient," *Revisiting Early Childhood Education*. New York: Holt, Rinehart & Winston, 1972.

Galambos, J. *Play & Playgrounds*. NAEYC. Washington DC, 1974.

Hirsch, L. ed. *The Block Book*. rev. NAEYC. Washington DC, 1984.

Jacobs, L. *Creative Dramatic, Washington*. Washington DC. ACEI, 1961.

Landeck, B. *Songs to Grow On*. New York: Wm. Sloane Assoc.

Mandelbaum, J., "Creative Dramatics in Early Childhood," *Young Children*. Jan. 1975.

Lasky, L. and Mukerji, R. *Art: Basic for Young Children*. NAEYC. Washington DC.

McDonald, D. *Music in our Lives: The Early Years*. NAEYC. Washington DC.

Montgomery, C. *What Difference Does Art Make in Young Children's Learning*. ECEC of New York.

Nixon, A. *A Child's Right to the Expressive Arts*. Washington DC.

Paley, V. *Bad Guys Don't Have Birthdays: Fantasy Play at Four*. Chicago: Univ. of Chicago Press, 1988.

Pitcher, E., et al. *Helping Young Children Learn*. Ohio: Charles Merrill, 1979.

Seeger, R. *American Folk Songs for Children*. New York: Doubleday, 1948.

Sponseller, D., ed. *Play as a Learning Medium*. NAEYC. Washington DC.

Learning Activities

In order to establish and maintain the kind of environment that will provide the greatest encouragement and support of the creative impulse in young children, there are a variety of activities and experiences we can undertake.

——1. To fully appreciate, understand, and enjoy the creative impulse in others, whether children or adults, we must first recognize, develop, and enjoy our own creativity. Take a course in using any creative art material. Use, experiment, and enjoy, alone or with fellow staff members, the art materials you provide for the children. Don't worry about making anything, just "mess about" with clay, paint, collage, woodwork, sand, soapsuds, etc. Play with a variety of manipulative materials such as pegboards, tables, blocks, etc.

——2. Using ideas from the art readings and your own feelings, plan for art activities to enhance children's creativity in tempera painting, finger painting, collage, printing, and clay. Observe and record children's reactions.

——3. Observe and record any instances of children's creative behavior in the classroom, either spontaneous or as a reaction to specially planned activities such as new ways of using collage, building, dramatic play.

——4. Identify, find, and place in the housekeeping area, a variety of unstructured materials that children can use to further their dramatic play. Observe and see if the play becomes increasingly complex and lasts longer for individual children and for group play.

——5. Find and place in the housekeeping center clothing and equipment that will help children explore new roles, i.e. uniform hats or stethoscopes.

——6. Plan and carry out activities in which children can make and use instruments such as drums, simple horns, and rhythm sticks. Allow children to explore the sounds these instruments make as well as to experience using them in a group and to accompany voice and piano.

——7. Use different varieties of music - through records, instruments, and talented adults - to encourage children to move with and without additional props, such as scarves, etc.

——8. Set up new ways of using ordinary materials, such as painting on different textures and out of doors, playing house under the trees, etc. Observe and record children's reactions.

——9. Read and then encourage children to act out familiar stories, providing simple props to encourage their dramatization.

——10. Explore poetry for yourself and then read some to children. Experiment with writing haiku and cinquaine poems with fellow staff and with the children.

——11. Visit and record observations of young children in some special creative arts program to observe creativity in children and the materials, activities, and teacher behavior that seem to encourage this creativity. Make provisions to discuss observations and ideas with fellow staff.

——12. Identify and list from your own experiences, observations, and readings any activities, materials, and adult behavior that inhibits or even destroys children's creative impulses.

——13. Make a list of children's opportunities to explore, create, and experiment over the course of a week in school. Identify any children you feel are exceptionally free to develop their creative impulse. Identify any children who seem unable to relax and enjoy using un-structured materials. Plan activities and develop personal interactions that will encourage such children to gain the confidence to explore and experiment and try new "ways" of play.

Other Related Learning Resources and Activities
(Fill in your own resources.)

_____

_____

_____

_____

_____

_____

_____

_____

_____

Competency Goal III

TO SUPPORT SOCIAL AND EMOTIONAL DEVELOPMENT AND PROVIDE POSITIVE GUIDANCE.

Functional Areas:
8. Self
9. Social
10. Guidance.

"What you think of me, I'll think of me; and what I think of me, I will be." This is what feeling good about oneself is all about.

From the time we are born, as we relate to the world around us - the people, the place, the things that make up our individual worlds - we are gradually developing our sense of self. The self that we know is the reflection we see in people's reactions to us. The first, most important, and most lasting of these reactions comes from the people who care for us as infants and children. As we grow, we carry this first impression of ourselves into a larger and larger world. First the world of our home, then of other children, classrooms, schools, and finally the adult world with its relationships with other adults, work, and work activities. Babies learn that they have an identity separate from their mother's or first caregiver's and that they have a body that exists separately from their mother's. As she or he meets baby's physical needs, responds to their reactions of pain and pleasure, the mother or first caregiver is establishing very basic ways in which the children will understand themselves. Do they feel loved? Can they trust their environment to meet their needs? Do they see themselves as people who can bring pleasure to others? Can they express love and affection, and can they reach out to those who care for them for help and love? As children grow and meet a widening circle of adults and other children, they carry the results of these first interactions with them. Do they look to other adults as being friendly people who will support them and enjoy being with them? Do they see other children as people who will join them in an exploration of their world? Do they see themselves, as they grow, as belonging to a group in society that is considered to be of value to society at large, with privileges and responsibilities within that society? If children find positive answers to these questions as they grow, they will see themselves as functioning, responsible members of the society in which they live.

As teachers of young children, we need to understand the foundations on which children can build positive feelings about themselves and awareness of their individual strengths, capabilities, and sense of worth. We need to understand that young children from birth are building a negative or positive understanding of who they are that will affect their entire adjustment, their ability to play, to learn, and to communicate. The older children grow, the harder it is for them to understand and internalize different ways of seeing themselves and to change their self-image from a negative to a positive orientation.

Teachers of young children have a great responsibility in this area of development. The children we teach are very young and their views of themselves are not fully established. Through what they see and do, children can be helped to increase their awareness of their worth and competence as doers and thinkers. By the type of relationships we establish with the children and with their parents, we can support the child's positive feelings of self-worth. We can set up a physical environment in which children can experience success, learn to accept and understand their own feelings, and develop opportunities for positive, happy, and enjoyable interactions with other human beings.

Essential to helping children maintain and/or develop a positive self-image is children's awareness of the consistency of our acceptance of each of them. As children realize they can rely on their teacher's support and affection, they can turn their energies toward their inner growth and development. Growing up means moving through new and unchartered areas, and human beings need a sense of support, of not being alone. Mature individuals have their own sense of self on which to rely but the young are in the process of developing this sense of self and must have the support of others.

Children who are sure of their share of the teacher's concern, acceptance, and affection have the courage to try new activities and put their abilities to the test. Their failures will not be allowed to devastate them, and their successes will be acknowledged. Since they are sure of their "share" of the teacher, each child will also be able to acknowledge other children's right to their "fair share." Energy does not need to be spent getting the teacher's attention. Children see themselves reflected in a consistently positive adult mirror, and they do not have to compete with other children mentally or physically for this awareness on the part of the teacher. They sense, too, that their teacher's acceptance, awareness, and support will not depend on what they do or do not do. The teacher does not praise or blame or withdraw support on the basis of performance. Some behavior is not acceptable, limits are always set on behavior that can harm the individual child or other children or adults - but each child should be accepted at all times.

This is one of our major responsibilities as teachers and it is easier said than done. To feel comfortable and accepting of other human beings, we need to develop awareness of our own worth as individuals. Through observation, introspection, and readings, we can begin to understand how the self develops in children and perhaps identify aspects of our own self-concepts. We, too, need the acceptance and support of others around us, such as fellow staff, administrators and family. We need to understand and respect our own cultural heritage and that of the families whose children we teach. It is in a program where the sense of teacher acceptance of fellow human beings is a stable aspect of the environment that we will find the sense of support and affection flowing in both directions. The network of positive human interactions provides the framework for real teaching. Children teach the teacher how to identify and meet their developmental needs, and teachers, trusted by children, can help children learn to meet the demands of group living.

Children who feel comfortable with themselves, who see themselves reflected positively by the actions and feelings of the adults and children around them are laying the foundation for a healthy personality - a person who will function effectively and with satisfaction in this world.

Resources

The following readings contain information and ideas that will help us understand and therefore support the development of a healthy personality in young children.

Axline, V. *Dibs, In Search of Self.* New York: Random House, 1966

Axline, V. *Play Therapy.* New York: Houghton Mifflin, 1947.

Frieberg, S. *The Magic Years.* New York: Scribner & Sons, 1959.

Hymes, J. *The Child Under 6.* New Jersey: Prentice Hall, 1968.

Mussen, Conger and Kagan. *Child Development and Personality.* 4th ed. New York: Harper & Row, 1974.

Neuman, Susan, Ph.D. and Panoff, Renee. *Exploring Feelings.* Atlanta: Humanics Limited, 1983.

Read, K.,Gardner, B. and Mahler, P. *Early Childhood Programs: A Laboratory for Human Relations.* 8th ed. New York: Holt, Rinehart & Winston, 1986.

Rose, Angie, Ph.D. and Weiss, Lynn, Ph.D. *Freedom to Grow.* Atlanta: Humanics Limited, 1984.

Segal, Marilyn, Ph.D. and Adcock, Don, Ph.D. *Feelings.* Atlanta: Humanics Limited, 1987.

COMPETENCY GOAL III
FUNCTIONAL AREA 8 - SELF

In order to help children develop a positive sense of self, we must build an environment of acceptance and support in which children can develop a sense of self worth as a boy or girl, as a member of their families, of their ethnic group, and as competent individuals within the school community.

As teachers, we must help children accept themselves as male or female. Children need to be aware of and comfortable about their sexual identity, not inhibited or resentful. Children also need to feel that they are accepted and supported by their families. By helping parents and other caregivers understand their children's developmental needs, we can help children accept and enjoy their place in their families.

The family unit, in whatever form it exists, is also a part of the community in terms of ethnicity and function. Children need to feel that they, too, are a part of their community as members of an ethnic-cultural group through their family identity and as members of their classroom. The program they attend must demonstrate its positive acceptance of differing cultural heritages as being an asset to community life. The program, through the teachers, must also develop children's understanding of the life and work styles of the community in which it exists.

Since children's understandings are founded on concrete experiences, children need to prove to themselves their ability to function effectively by learning to make choices and seeing themselves as competent members of the community of children. Children develop this self-awareness by learning what they are capable of doing, learning, and achieving. They learn to control their bodies through large and small muscle activities, to develop a sense of mastery as they are allowed sufficient time to practice, incorporate, and perfect physical and intellectual skills into the development of new abilities. Since young children are still developing a sense of self, they should not be subjected to situations in which they must compete with other children, and possibly fail in relation to them. They then see themselves reflected negatively as unable to perform or produce. When they are encouraged and supported in competing with themselves, they can build a realistic awareness of themselves based on their own capacities.

Functional Area 8

Self Checklist*

As teachers, we can work in a variety of ways to help children develop a positive sense of self.

—1. We help children grow toward positive identification as competent members within the child community by:

- ☐ Never involving children in competitive situations, encouraging them to compete only with themselves. For example: "You worked hard on that shoelace." *Never,* "Johnny can tie his laces, everyone."
- ☐ Offering support until children show they no longer need it and can manage on their own.
- ☐ Always showing children that help is there if they need it.
- ☐ Making no comparisons between children.
- ☐ Making no judgments about children's work or activities, i.e. "good eater, good painter."
- ☐ Commenting on each child's real success, such as length of attention, quality of emotion. For example: "You really worked hard." "You did it yourself and you had fun."
- ☐ Commenting on children's likes and dislikes. For example: "John doesn't like red. Blue is his favorite."
- ☐ Avoiding harsh or rejecting tones of voice. For example: "John, you need to come now." Not, "Get over here."

—2. We plan an environment that can challenge a child to move forward in levels of skill by:

- ☐ Providing materials of increasing difficulty, like puzzles and various sized beads and pegs, always starting from the child's level of mastery.
- ☐ Providing opportunities to use materials, so children can reinforce their sense of mastery without pressure to move forward all the time.
- ☐ Providing an atmosphere that supports experimentation and creativity and does not criticize mistakes and failures.
- ☐ Providing support to finish a hard job when we know a child can do it, but may be scared; our presence may be enough support.

*This checklist may be copied for your portfolio.

☐ Repeating activities many times so children can achieve mastery in skill and understanding. For example: Give children opportunities to use scissors over and over until they can cut and then let them use that skill to achieve other skills - cutting one kind of shape or selected pictures. Give children opportunities to plant many kinds of seeds so their concrete experiences lead to real understanding.

——3. We are aware of an deal constructively with individual children's style and capacities to learn by:

☐ Being aware of appropriate behavior at given age levels, birth to six years old, and viewing growth on a continuum and using this knowledge in planning all aspects of the curriculum.

☐ Understanding each child's own growth levels and showing this by understanding and accepting the child's behavior. For example: A child sucks her thumb for security; we give her a lot of support and she is doing it less.

☐ Maintaining on-going records of each child so we can match our expectations to the child's growth.

☐ Maintaining records so we can evaluate each child's growth over the year.

——4. We help children grow towards a positive identity as a boy or girl by:

☐ Not making statements such as "boys don't, little girls do."

☐ Accepting children's exploration of varying roles, without comment, such as boys holding dolls, girls building airplanes, etc. Encouraging parents of both sexes to visit and, by their presence, model male and female roles.

☐ Working with parents to help them deal constructively with children's sexuality.

☐ Answering questions honestly, but not volunteering information beyond what children ask, concerning sex roles.

☐ Searching out adult community workers of both sexes and requesting that they visit and share their work roles with the children.

☐ Searching for appropriate books showing boys and girls engaged in a variety of activities without regard to sex.

☐ Finding concrete examples of male and female animals and the maternal and paternal roles; we do not need to do more than expose children to existence of these roles.

☐ Encouraging children to fulfill their potential so they have a positive sense of self, regardless of sex.

☐ Indicating by words and actions, an awareness that a feeling of self-worth means that children accept themselves and their sex as well; being aware that feelings of self-worth are the foundation of a good sense of self.

☐ Showing by our own way of living and by verbal example that we are comfortable in our own sex roles. Dressing comfortably, discussing our own roles as parents, etc.

——5. We help children grow towards positive identification as members of their families by: Being aware of the effect of the child's placement in the family, i.e. "the baby" or "the big boy."

☐ Encouraging children to try new age-related roles, putting a family "baby" together with a younger child to act in helpful role, etc.

56

☐ Being aware that one of the most important tasks of early education is to help each child become the best person their families would like them to become in terms of self-realization.

☐ Accepting children's feelings about their family members and their own family situation. Sharing children's triumphs with their families, i.e. "John learned to cut today."

☐ Presenting a variety of activities around holidays so the preschoolers' contributions to their family celebrations can rank with that of the other children in the family, i.e. perhaps a photo of the child in a frame the child has painted. Children can make cranberry sauce and colored wrapping paper for the container. Keeping in touch with parents and helping them with concrete suggestions to accept their own child's behavior at the different levels of development, by modeling effective ways of working with children and inviting parents to observe the group and see other children.

☐ Providing opportunities for children to think about family relationships, using a well-planned housekeeping area, puppets, pictures, doll house, doll furniture and dolls, and books and stories that explore different family relationships and different family models.

——6. We help children develop positive identification as members of their ethnic/cultural groups by:

☐ Providing books, pictures, and toys that reflect ethnic balance of the group.

☐ Accepting and encouraging parents and other community members to visit, volunteer, and be a part of the program at regular intervals. They can share their backgrounds, songs, foods, and holidays with the children.

☐ Planning in class for cooking experiences that reflect the children's backgrounds.

☐ Planning with a nutritionist and cooks to include foods in the nutrition program that are familiar to children and to introduce new foods.

☐ Incorporating songs and stories of different ethnic groups into the program in an easy and appropriate way. Using folk songs and stories of interest to all children of different ethnic groups, such as *Snowy Day, Rosa-too-little, Gilberto and the Wind,* etc.

☐ Incorporating commonly used expressions and greetings - i.e. names of classroom materials, words, and games - in the child's native language into class usage.

☐ Incorporating music and typical instruments and folk songs of other countries into the music of the program.

☐ Incorporating the various holidays from the different cultures of the children into the holiday plans of the program and using parents to help carry our these plans.

☐ **If we are competent as a bilingual specialist,** we will incorporate both languages into all the activities that help children develop positive identification as members of their ethnic group.

Resources

The following reading resources will be helpful in learning more about the ways to identify and support different aspects of a child's developing sense of self.

Bilingual and Bicultural Resources

Escopedo, T. *Early Childhood Bilingual Education, A Hispanic Perspective.* NAEYC. Washington DC.

Glass, P. *Songs and Stories of Afro-America.* New York: Gosset & Dunlap, 1971.

Hale-Benson, J. *Black Children: Their roots, culture and learning styles.* rev. Baltimore: Johns Hopkins Press, 1986.

Landeck, B. *Echoes of Africa.* New York: McKay, 1969.

Lubeck, S. *Sandbox Society, Early Education in Black and White America. A Comparative Ethnography.* Philadelphia: The Falmer Press, Taylor & Francis Inc. 1985.

A Better Chance to Learn: Bilingual, Bicultural Education, U.S. Commission on Civil Rights, Clearinghouse Publications #51, May 1975

Exceptional Child

Brucker, D. *Early Education of at-risk and handicapped infants, toddlers and preschool children.* Glenview, Illinois: Scott Foreman, 1986.

Cook, R. and Arbruster. *Adopting Early Childhood Curricula: Suggestions for Meeting Special Needs.* St. Louis: Mosby, 1986.

Self

Baker and Fane *Understanding and Guiding Young Children.* 2nd ed. New Jersey: Prentice Hall, 1972.

Cohen, D., Stern, V. and Balaban, N. *Observing and Recording the Behavior of Young Children.* 3rd ed. New York: Teachers College Press, Columbia University, 1983.

Ginot. *Teacher and Child.* New York: MacMillan, 1972.

Kiester, D. *Who Am I?.* Durham: Learning Institute of North Carolina, 1973.

Paley, V.G. *Mollie is Three: Growing Up In School.* Chicago: University of Chicago Press, 1986.

Samuels, S. *Enhancing Self-Concept in Early Childhood.* New York: Human Sciences Press, 1977.

Sprung, B. *Non-Sexist Early Childhood Education.* New York: Womens' Actions Alliance, 1974.

Wardle, F. "Are You Sensitive to Interracial Children's Special Identity Needs?" *Young Children.* January,1987. Washington DC.

Warren, R. *Caring; Supporting Children's Growth.* NAEYC. Washington DC. 1977.

Learning Activities

The following activities will help us as teachers develop understanding and techniques for supporting the growth of children's positive self-concept.

—-1. Plan and carry out four activities, using a different technique for fostering children's positive sense of self. These activities can include cooking, taping songs and stories, making silhouettes and books about families and favorite things.

—-2. Study a variety of children's books. Select five books which reflect a positive image of a child's ethnic group and write a short annotation of each book. Read each book to the children, formulate questions for discussion and keep a record of children's responses. Plan an activity involving art, music, or dramatic play related to the story.

—-3. Develop an annotated booklists of children's stories relating to the development of a healthy sense of self. Note, in writing, the children's reactions to selected stories from this list. (See Page 43)

—-4. Develop games relating to a healthy sense of self by using pictures, dramatic play, color slides, and videotaping. Note, in writing, the children's reactions.

—-5. Develop materials to encourage children to experience a wide variety of roles in their daily classroom living. Note children's reactions of roles in their daily classroom living. Note children's reactions and develop a pictorial record of children engaged in activities. (See page 46)

—-6. From libraries, magazines, and visits to museums, select pictures and prints of appropriate works of poetry, songs, and music by artists of different ethnic and cultural groups to use in class with preschool children. Make note, in writing or through pictures, of children's reactions to these materials. Assemble a bibliography of such works of art, poetry, and music to share with fellow staff members.

—-7. Plan for parents and community members representing different ethnic, cultural, and community groups to visit in class and participate in activities with children. Keep a pictorial and written record to which children can refer, i.e. experience charts, children's dictated stories.

——8. Plan for class to visit areas in the community relating to different ethnic groups and keep records for children's use as indicated above.

——9. Keep on-going records of children's behavior in relation to their developing abilities and feelings of competency, by noting how often a child participates happily in a group activity and initiates positive contacts.

If you are working towards a Bilingual Specialization, it is important to:

——10. Relate to children in their own language, concerning their feelings, behaviors, skills, and activities.

——11. Encourage children to express their feelings and concerns in their own language and in English if they can.

Other Related Learning Resources and Activities
(Fill in your own resources.)

_____

_____

_____

_____

_____

_____

_____

_____

_____

_____

_____

_____

_____

_____

Functional Areas:
9. Social

In order to feel happy about coming to school, both adults and children need to feel comfortable with each other and sure of their place as important members of the group. Each person needs to understand and be able to share thoughts and feelings with the others. We all need to know that there are people in our classroom who are glad to see us and that we will all feel satisfied and that our day was well spent when we leave.

Teachers must remember that the love and trust given to them by children also helps them live and work with satisfaction. Loving and caring always go two ways. When teachers help children feel comfortable with their friends, feeling they are a part of the group, they are using many of the skills and competencies we have already discussed.

Children who see adults talk to each other and express concern about the feelings of others will learn to do the same. Children learn that a push hurts another child, that other children need a chance to see, touch, and play, that we know how good each child feels when a job is completed, how sad it is when Mommy is not home or a favorite toy is broken. As we accept and acknowledge the reality of children's feelings, we help children understand those feelings and deal with them realistically and responsibly in ways that prevent harm to self and to others, but provide needed release from excessive stress and tension.

For many children, coming to a preschool program represents one of their first steps outside the social group of their own family. Under the guidance of a supportive and accepting teacher, they meet groups of other children who form what is often their first peer group. Since young children are necessarily concerned first of all with themselves (Will their needs be met in this new place? Will others like them? Will they find friends?), these are the first concerns we teachers must meet. We must set up an environment so each child is sure of an individual place within it. There need to be cubbies labelled for each child, attendance charts that help children become aware of each member of the group. Children are provided with opportunities to do interesting and satisfying things together, such as eating, cooking, and going on trips. Most important of all are the teachers who are aware of each member of the class. Children watch closely to see how we react to other children. Do we get mad about accidents or mistakes, do we provide comfort when someone bumps herself or misses Mommy? Children take note of how we respond to their own needs, "Does teacher really listen when I talk, does she/he see how hard the job was?" The children who know that they have established working lines of communication between themselves and the teachers who care for them will be able to allow others to establish the same kind of communication. They gain a sense of trust towards teachers; teachers accept them, meet their needs, and enjoy them as individuals, therefore, they can wait for their turn to participate in an activity. They know their turn will come. They can share the teacher's attention with others and accept the fact that others' needs will be met as well as their own. Every time we teachers solve a problem of group living in a way that acknowledges the needs of the individuals involved, we are teaching all the children the value of group cooperation. By supporting and cooperating with fellow staff and other adults, we set an example to the children of supportive and nurturing group living. Children "learn what they live" and as adults love and care for their growth, so will they learn to love and care for each other. In many ways, we help children take the first developmental steps toward their role as functioning members in a democratic society.

As teachers, therefore, we have a major responsibility to provide the supportive, relaxed environments in which children learn to move from being absorbed in themselves to being aware of and comfortable with other children. As they learn to play with and relate to other children, they add new dimensions to their own learning and growing. We the teachers are the first and most important friends children will have in school.

Functional Area 9

Social Checklist*

Teachers set the tone for the children's year - they will be liked, accepted, and helped, and then encouraged to like, help and accept others. We do this by:

——1. Setting up an environment in which children make positive steps towards cooperative group living. Guiding emotional and social behavior to reinforce positive group interaction and help children develop skills in group living by:

☐ Praising with reasons - praising the job, not the child.

☐ Praising (verbal or non-verbal - a pat, a hug, a nod) to reward behavior.

☐ Reflecting children's feelings - giving them words for their feelings. For example:"Tell him you want it.""He is sad because he misses Mommy.""She is crying because her finger hurts.""She is angry because you hit her head with the end of the block.""He is angry because he was reading the book and you took it away."

☐ Encouraging children to talk about their feelings. For example: "Tell him you need a turn soon."

☐ Treating conflict situations as problems to be solved. For example: "You both need a truck, now what can we do?"

☐ Providing limits with alternative possible choices. For example: "You may not hit him, you may hit the punching bag."

☐ Verbalizing description and consequences of social behavior. For example: "You both cleaned the tables, now we can all eat."

☐ Modeling positive social interactions.

☐ Knowing children and waiting to see if they can solve their own problems.

——2. Helping children develop skills in cooperative relationships by:

☐ Working cooperatively on a job with an individual child.

☐ Involving a shy child in an activity with yourself as partner.

☐ Planning activities to encourage cooperation, first in small groups, i.e. two to wash paint brushes, set table, rock in a rocking boat together, and run an errand.

*This checklist may be copied for your portfolio.

☐ Avoiding competition and comparisons among the children in the classroom.

☐ Planning well-organized centers of interest in the classroom.

☐ Arranging for well-planned activities where children can be involved and still socialize - crayoning at a table, playing in the doll corner, playing at sand and water tables, sitting and looking at books together.

☐ Encouraging children to choose companions. Free-choice activity times allow children to choose those with whom they want to play, etc.

——3. Staying aware of the relationships between children in the class. In a group where adults and children enjoy the quality of their life together, children relate easily to others, and little hostility of friction is evident as they use materials and equipment.

☐ Children demonstrate their concern for each other by seeking help from adults when a friend is in need and participate easily in activities that demonstrate concern for a child who is sick or absent.

☐ Children accept visitors easily, making casual, friendly inquiries, and include them in classwork or ignore them when involved in class activities. They will ask a visitor's help if the teacher indicates acceptance of the visitor and if they need help.

——4. We plan the program of activities for the children to include opportunities for playing and working together and sharing experiences and responsibilities with adults in a spirit of enjoyment as well as for the sake of social development. As teachers we:

☐ Express enjoyment by tone of voice and involvement in the activities in the classroom.

☐ Verbalize satisfaction in being together "That was fun; we all worked hard." "I love snow, don't you?"

☐ Take part in many activities in ways that encourage children to do the same, i.e. joining in singing, talking with children at meals.

☐ Take part in outdoor activities like swinging, digging, pulling wagons, etc., to share the fun and encourage children's participation. Always be ready to yield your place to an interested child.

☐ Join children during routines such as cleanup so they get a sense of cooperation in group living. "Let's clean up; I'll work with you."

☐ Verbalize good feelings about other teachers. For example: "I am so glad you are back, Mrs. Jones."

☐ Show children we know they will accept our support or special treatment of any given child when they know they will also be cared for and supported in their time of need. For example: "Susan really needs a cuddle, she is sad because her Mommy is sick." "Poor John, he really hurt his head. "

If we are competent as Bilingual Specialists, we:

——5. Understand different social roles and expectations among bilingual children in their home and school settings and help children cope with these differ

Resources

The following readings, as well as those listed for previous competencies, will be useful in helping us understand the process of developing positive social interaction in a group of young children.

Curry, N. *The Feeling Child: Affective Development Reconsidered.* New York: Haworth Press, 1986.

Goffin, S. "Cooperative Behaviors: They Need Our Support" *Young Children.* January 1987. NAEYC. Washington DC.

Griffin, E.F. *Island of Childhood: Education in the Special World of Nursery School.* New York: Teachers College Press, Columbia Univ. 1982.

Read, K.H., Gardner, B. and Mahler, P. *Early Childhood Programs: A Laboratory for Human Relationships.* 8th ed. New York: Holt, Rinehart & Winston, 1986.

Wolf, D.P. *Connecting: Friendship in the Lives of Young Children and Their Teachers.* Redmond, Washington: Exchange Press Inc. 1986.

Learning Activities

Carrying out some of the following learning activities will help teachers maintain an environment in which they can support and encourage children's increasing capacity to live and work cooperatively.

——1. Plan (in writing) and carry out a variety of activities in which children can play cooperatively in small and large groups.

——2. Plan (in writing) and carry out activities for small groups of children to work together in the different centers of interest in the room .

——3. Select list and use 15 storybooks that deal with children making new friends, having good times together, cooperating on a special activity, etc. Note children's reactions.

——4. For one week, keep an on-going record of one's child's social interactions in class - positive contacts initiated by each child with another child or adult, contacts responded to by child, negative contacts initiated by child with other children, and negative contacts responded to by child. What does this tell you about the child's needs and strengths? How can you support the child's growth?

——5. Select songs that help children learn each other's names and interact with each other in creative dramatic plays. Keep a record of the songs and activities that work well with children.

If you are working towards a Bilingual Specialization:

——6. Use both languages to help children participate in small and large group activities.

——7. Use a variety of bilingual stories and songs to help children work and play happily and comfortably together.

Other Related Learning Resources and Activities
(Fill in your own resources.)

_____

_____

_____

_____

_____

_____

_____

_____

_____

_____

_____

_____

_____

_____

_____

_____

COMPETENCY GOAL III
FUNCTIONAL AREA 10 - Guidance and Discipline

Human beings need a sense of structure in which to live cooperatively without unnecessary tensions. Classrooms should be happy places. Adults and children should look forward to the days they spend together. They should come away from school each day feeling a little bit better about themselves than they did the day before - children because they are learning, growing, and knowing more about their world and themselves, and grownups because they are effectively supporting and enhancing the growth and development of the children in their charge and, in the process, learning to understand themselves better.

In such classrooms, children and adults understand the daily routines, the sequence of the day's activities, and the limits necessary for comfortable group living. Teachers have expectations of children's behavior that take into account their level of attention, skills, need for movement, ability to work cooperatively, and need for concrete experiences.

Just as a good learning environment depends on our ability to organize the physical environment, it also depends on our ability to establish and maintain effective and relaxed patterns of group living.

We need to plan carefully both for the timing and content in our daily programs. We plan with the other adults in the classroom to maintain careful supervision of all activities, appropriate sequence of active and quiet activities and meaningful curriculum, orderly transitions, and appropriate time for each activity. We are aware of our individual responsibilities in implementing these plans and work cooperatively and in a supportive manner with children and fellow workers.

A good place to be; a good place for you and me. That is how children and adults should feel about the classrooms in which they live and work. Feelings like this don't just happen. Teachers create such happy places with children by developing caring and accepting relationships with everyone in the classroom and by using effective skills in guidance and discipline to keep life running smoothly day by day.

Closely related to children's emotional and social development is their growing need for and achieving of independence. Young children must be carefully supported and guided in their growth towards independence and autonomy. As we care for them, we must help them become aware of their increasing ability to do things for themselves by establishing an environment in which self-help skills are fostered and in which mistakes and inability, at times, to function at the expected level are accepted as part of the usual growing process, not a matter for blame or shame.

It is good for teachers of young children to try to learn new skills, to experience firsthand the process of acquiring new skills. It is also important for us to try to understand the reality of children's feelings by trying to remember our own feelings as children and understand how children's thinking influences what they can understand and what they feel. Children often base their perfectly logical and completely inaccurate conclusions on very incomplete evidence. They are too young to have gained the experience and knowledge to help them see beyond the present realities. At this age, they know only what they perceive.

Young children are enveloped by their feelings. They hate completely and love completely, and their complete involvement with themselves makes it hard for them to see beyond their own awareness of their feelings. Caring, supportive adults will help them understand reality and become aware of the limits of reality in terms of their needs, feelings, and capacities.

Since children, in the beginning, only know themselves, they also view the world around them as if they were the center of everything. They think that everything that happens stems from them. Children are aware only of their own feelings of hunger, pleasure, and pain. Their sadness and joy fill the world. As they grow older and experience the frustrations of group living in family and in school, they believe their anger fills the world, too, and that when they say, "I hate you, go away," this statement actually has the power to make you go away.

Children grab something because they are only aware of their own needs. Parents and teachers, by example, need to help children understand that their own actions influence the way others feel and behave. By talking about labeling, and identifying feelings, we help children understand what is happening to themselves and, equally important, to others.

Functional Area 10

Guidance and Discipline Checklist *

As teachers of young children, we must help them develop capacities to cope independently with their world, meet their own needs when possible, and also know when to seek outside help and support. If we are to be effective in guiding children, we will be aware of much of the following information and will use it in daily interactions with children.

——1. We are aware of the basic process by which children learn to trust the world in which they live and the people with whom they live. We will show each child we can be relied on to take care of them by:

- ☐ Guiding children through precepts of positive discipline by telling children what they can do, what they can't, giving them choices they can make, etc.
- ☐ Being consistent about class routines.
- ☐ Setting safety limits.
- ☐ Knowing how to be calm in an emergency.
- ☐ Protecting child's rights and those of other children .
- ☐ Helping children control unsocial behavior, "You can't kick John, and he can't hit you."
- ☐ Accepting each child's needs as well as those of others and keeping the need to share, wait, and take turns, limited until the children are sure that they trust the school environment. For example: "This is your car, you brought it from home," "It is your turn to ride now."

——2. We help children learn to be considerate of the rights of others by protecting their legitimate individual rights.

——3. We are aware of individual children's patterns of dependent and independent behavior. We do this by:

- ☐ Observing individual children closely so we can intervene to help a child at the best time.
- ☐ Offering help when we know through observation that the child can't manage on his own.
- ☐ Offering or giving help without negative comments, such as, "You are old enough to do it yourself."
- ☐ Knowing that when children seek help, they need it even if it is only the support of the adult's physical presence or observation, i.e. "I'll watch you as you climb."

*This checklist may be copied for your portfolio

☐ Giving help and talk about the fact that we all need help at times. Teachers should ask for and accept help at times, too.

☐ Being free and comfortable about giving emotional support when children show they need it verbally and non-verbally. For example: Children come and lean on teachers or hold on to them, knowing they will be patted, held, etc.

☐ Preparing children for what lies ahead so that familiarity lessens fear. For example: an eye examination, a dental check-up.

☐ Trying to share with parents the reality of children's fears and children's need to know what to expect in their daily lives.

☐ Stress that within the limits of school, we will help children achieve their rightful goals and that "might does not make right" in the ordered society of the classroom.

——4. We help children understand that they can make mistakes and will not be criticized ridiculed or punished. As teachers we:

☐ Comment on actions, not on children. "Oh, the milk spilled," *not* "You were sloppy."

☐ Focus on the remedy and prevention, not on the error. "Oh, here is a sponge; let's clean it up."

☐ Show we can make mistakes, too, and accept help and correction. For example: "Oh, I did make a mess with the milk," "Yes, I did put the square in the wrong box."

——5. We help all children realize that they are valued for themselves as individuals. As teachers we:

☐ Do not make comparisons between one child and another. *Never* compare family members. For example: "Your sister is such a good runner, you can run fast if you try."

☐ Compare a child only with him or herself, not with other children. For example: "You can climb so high now; remember when you could only get to there."

☐ Show children we will follow through on individual requests where possible.

☐ Never discuss children or their feelings within their hearing unless we include them directly in the discussion.

☐ Show children we have confidence in the essential value of each of them by expecting them to live constructively within the group. For example:

Children can wait for recognition. They know the teacher cares for and knows each one of them.

Children easily express their feelings of sympathy, affection, pleasure, and hurt.

——6. We accept the reality of children's feelings. Some indications are:

☐ We establish supportive relationships with children who are upset.

☐ We do not isolate a child having a temper tantrum from all adult contact.

☐ We name and reflect a child's angry feelings. For example: "I know you really want the truck." "I know you are very angry because she hurt you." "I know you want Daddy to stay."

☐ We name and reflect happy, satisfied feelings. For example: "You are so glad Mom is home again." "You worked hard and you finished all by yourself." "It's your turn and you really waited."

☐ We comfort children even with a slight hurt so they get the message that we care.

——7. We are aware, as teachers are, that in new situations, children need a lot of repeated reassurances. We provide this support by:

☐ Reassuring statements. For example: "We'll keep your truck right here in the cubby." "Mommy is at work right now, but she'll be here for you after snack." "The bus will be right here to take you home."

☐ Cleanup routines that are the same daily so children get to know what to expect of the physical environment.

☐ Consistent reactions so children learn what to expect of their teachers. For example: "Oh, the paint spilled; let's clean it up." "I'm so glad to see you today."

——8. We share children's pleasures, see the fun in classroom situations, and can laugh at ourselves. As teachers we:

☐ Recognize the fun in splashing soap suds, running through leaves, etc.

☐ Wear clothing or smocks that encourage our own active participation in classroom activities.

☐ Dress up on occasion and join in an activity, even if we look funny. Take part in dramatic play, circle games, and songs, without being self-conscious.

☐ Read stories with expression and involvement when appropriate; show a little bit of the actor that is in all of us.

——9. We create an atmosphere in which people can express feelings, in positive and negative ways that do not harm others.

——10. We always try to accept the reality of a child's feelings. For example: "You are afraid of the dog, aren't you?", *never,* "There is nothing to be scared of.", or "You are angry at your brother, aren't you?", *never,* "No one hates their baby brother.", etc.

——11. We talk freely about our feelings. For example: "I feel so good today; the sun is so warm." "I am so glad you are back; I missed you." "You scared me when you stood on the swing; I can't let you get hurt." "I do not like it when you try to kick; it makes me feel angry, too." "I really hurt myself on that sharp edge; let's fix it."

——12. We put words to children's feelings for them and accept their expressions of feelings, always keeping the expression within the limits of group living. For example: "It's o.k. to be afraid; I won't let them hurt you." "It's o.k. to be afraid, lots of people worry about the dentist; I'll stay with you." "I know you are angry; he hurt your feelings." "You can kick at the ball, but you cannot kick at Jane, I won't let her kick you and I won't let you kick her."

——13. We help children channel their negative, disruptive behaviors into safe channels by:

☐ Finding safe outlets for aggression, such as water, play, and clay.

☐ Allowing a reasonable lack of conformity. "John is really sad today and just can't listen to the story."

☐ Removing angry children from situations they can't handle and give them a substitute activity. Allowing tense children to stay away from the story circle if they are quiet or stay close to the other teacher, etc.

——14. We always offer our support and protection. For example: "I'll hold your hand as you balance." "I'll stand here while you climb; I'll watch."

——15. We are aware that a child's intellectual, emotional, and social growth are based on their developing a sense of trust in the world of school. We should:
- ☐ Be aware that when distracted by unhappy feelings, insecurity, anger, etc., children cannot really be involved in teaching-learning activities.
- ☐ Make provisions for unhappy, upset children while maintaining reasonable living limits for the group.

——16. We encourage children to express feelings verbally - sad, mad, as well as glad.

——17. We show children, by accepting them as they are, that we are concerned for and understand them and will let them be themselves. For example: Teachers reflect children's feelings to them; "I know you want Mommy so much." or "I know you want to ride that truck." Teachers set the limits of reality so children can understand them; "Mommy has to go to work; I'll stay with you." or "John has his turn now; you'll have one later."

——18. We should be aware that children need love and concern constantly so they can spend their energies on learning and growing and do not need to look for affection from every adult they meet. In such an environment, children seem relaxed and busy.

——19. We recognize verbally and non-verbally and only on an individual basis, children's successes in terms of skills, span of attention, and involvement and interest level. For example: "You really worked hard," or a pat on the shoulder.
- ☐ Lengthened span of attention is noted on children's records (ones kept privately by teachers for our own guidance in helping individual children).
- ☐ Children's learning of specific skills is noted as indicated above on school records when appropriate.

——20. We recognize the children's growing sense of initiative and responsibility by:
- ☐ Planning for children to use materials independently (See Competency Goals I and II).
- ☐ Planning for children to deepen dramatic play and create their own environments (See Competency Goals I and II).

——21. We comment on the job done, not on the children. For example: "You had a real rest today," *not,* "You are a good rester." "You are hungry today," *not,* "You are a good eater. "

——22. We encourage self-help skills, the ability to make choices, and independence in life in the classroom by:
- ☐ Providing materials and equipment suitable for the ages of the children in the class.
- ☐ Allowing and arranging for children to repeat activities until they master skills.
- ☐ Arranging all creative art materials so children can use them and replace them independently.
- ☐ Marking block shelves so children can take and replace blocks correctly.
- ☐ Making containers for toys so cleanup can be done by children independently.
- ☐ Arranging for children to help themselves in food service - setting tables, preparing certain foods, serving food independently in utensils children can handle, and cleaning up.
- ☐ Arranging for children to help set up cots or mats for rest and get their own bedding and nap toys.
- ☐ Arranging for children to help themselves in toileting, toothbrushing, etc.
- ☐ Arranging cleanup so children understand the routine and can help themselves so they realize it is an obligation of the total group. Provide sponges, buckets, mops, and

brushes (regular size with shortened handles) accessible to children for independent use.

☐ Arranging for children to have clothing fastenings they can learn to handle in doll corner, on smocks, and on clothing boards.

☐ Making waterproof smocks available to children to use independently for art work, water play, cooking, sand table, and dramatic play areas.

——23. We provide children with opportunities for active participation and independent choices by:

☐ Giving children regularly planned opportunities for active participation allowing for their direct involvement with materials. Each child mixes colors, tries with floats, etc.

☐ Giving children regular opportunities for making independent choices by planning for an adequate free-choice period with a large variety of activities using all areas of interest in the room.

☐ Providing learning activities that use different senses so that children can use their own efficient sense. For example: Children have chances to become aware of similarities and differences using sight, hearing, feeling, taste, and smell.

——24. As teachers we are aware that children achieve success and mastery and try for new skills when they are sure of adult acceptance and support. We take pride in child's independence.

For example, we say:

"I know the milk spilled this time: let's try again. I'll help you hold the pitcher steady."

"I won't let you fall; you can hold my hand." *Never,* "You're a big girl, you don't need help."

"You don't have to get wet (or finger paint, etc.) if you don't want to; why don't you stay right by me and just watch."

——25. The teacher is willing to give children time to grow and develop in their own time.

☐ Planning for needed adult help in maintaining flexibility in the program. For example: Not everyone has to go outside at the same time every day. "John is going to finish painting - he has really worked hard on it. He'll come out to the playground later."

☐ Giving children plenty of time to complete a job, etc.

——26. We establish a warm, nurturing, and supportive relationship with each child. We need to be emotionally responsive by:

☐ Using gentle physical contact - a pat, a tap, a hug, a hand on the cheek - to show children they are cared for and understood.

☐ Identifying feelings in simple words, "You are sad/glad." "You made the table really clean; what a hard job you did."

☐ Using smiles, eyes, and tone of voice to show children we know they are there, to keep their attention, to accept them and their contributions to group life.

☐ Helping children to establish non-verbal contact easily with us, such as leaning against us, holding our hands, and establishing eye contact with us.

☐ Using short sentences and simple words to explain feelings. "I know you feel sad; grandma will be here soon."

☐ Making each child in some way each day feel that we are aware of their presence. We watch their faces and expressions to understand them.

☐ Always being concerned about the effect on each child of any activity plan, etc.

27. We help children realize that each one has their share of the teacher's love, attention, and concern. As teachers, we:

☐ Respond on a one-to-one basis to each child every day.

☐ Communicate our warmth of feeling verbally by tone of voice.

☐ Communicate our warmth of feeling non-verbally.

☐ Select stories, songs, pictures, and materials that reflect children's emotions based on their needs. For example: child who has been hospitalized is shown stories about hospitals and is given medical uniforms, stethoscope, etc., to play with.

28. Children show they know they are loved by:

☐ Taking turns easily when they must.

☐ Accepting the reality of a shortage in the supply of materials if it does not happen consistently.

☐ Waiting easily for adult recognition at storytime, etc.

☐ Enjoying working with adults in a relaxed way, not trying to be teacher's partner all the time, etc.

☐ Not constantly reaching for teachers or for visible marks of their recognition and affection.

☐ Not seeking affection from casual visitors.

29. We understand that classroom control is based on good interpersonal relationships with the children and adults involved and on reasonable expectations of children's behavior. We exercise control without being threatening.

30. We know classroom limits are necessary for comfortable group living, basing our expectations of children's behavior on their age and development.

31. We avoid threatening or scaring. We give positive directions. For example: "We'll walk down this steep hill." "We'll hand John the big blocks."

32. We enforce limits without labeling the child good or bad. For example: "No one in this class may throw blocks." *Not,* "Good children don't throw, spit, etc."

33. We protect the basic orderliness of the situation but still let children use materials and equipment freely. Some indicators are:

☐ Teachers participate in cleanup and transition.

☐ Children select their play materials and equipment and use them in interesting and original ways.

☐ Room is arranged to maintain easy cleanup and storage.

34. We are aware of the limits imposed by age on children's ability to cope with group living and learning by:

☐ Keeping learning groups small. Avoiding taking turns unnecessarily and avoiding overexciting, too large group activity situations, too long bus rides, etc.

☐ Avoiding unreasonable demands, such as everyone sleeping at nap time, no talking on the bus, and finishing all food on the plate.

☐ Planning opportunities for individual exploration of materials, group-oriented games, demonstration and participation in a way consistent with children's ages. For example: Three-year-olds share less and do more parallel playing and are more oriented to the concrete experiences.

☐ Stating limits and rules in positive ways, ways that don't create blame but help children internalize the controls they need to function in a group. For example: "Sand stays in the sandbox." Not, "Don't dump the sand out." "We don't bite in this class." Not, "Good girls don't bite."

——35. We establish limits, showing by our behavior that we expect children to live within those limits because of our rapport with the group. We limit our demands for real and quick obedience to situations that are serious. For example: Where children's safety is concerned; "We must all cross the street now." "That bell says we must go out right now."

Resources

The following resources will help us, as teachers, understand how we can support children's sense of independence and autonomy. Some of these books are also listed under the Functional Areas of Self and Social since children's development of their sense of self, positive social behaviors, and teachers' positive guidance and discipline are very closely related.

Axline, V. *Dibs, In Search of Self.* New York. Ballantine Books, 1966.

Baker, K.R. *The Nursery School and Kindergarten.* 7th ed. New York: Holt, Rinehart & Winston, 1980.

Birckmayer, J. *Discipline Is Not a Dirty Word.* New York: Cooperative Extension, Cornell University.

Cherry, C. *Please Don't Sit on the Kids.* Belmont, California: Pitman Learning, 1983.

Church and Stone *Childhood and Adolescence.* 4th ed. New York: Random House, 1979.

Cohen, D., Stern, V. and Balaban. *Observing and Recording the Behavior of Young Children.* 3rd ed. New York: Teachers College Press, Columbia University, 1983.

Dreikurs, R. and Cassel, P. *Discipline Without Tears.* New York: Haworth Press, 1972.

Ginott, H. *Between Parent and Child.* New York: MacMillan, 1965.

Ginott, H. *Teacher and Child.* New York: MacMillan, 1972.

Glasser, W. *Reality Therapy.* New York: Harper & Row, 1965.

Hildebrand, V. *Guiding Young Children.* New York: MacMillan, 1978.

Honig, A. "Research in Review: Compliance, Control and Discipline" (Parts 1 and 2) *Young Children* 40(2) 5-58; 40(3) 47-52

Honig, A. "Stress and Coping With Children" (Parts 1 and 2) *Young Children*, May, 1986; July, 1986. NAEYC. Washington DC.

Keister, D. *Who Am I?* Durham, North Carolina: Durham Learning Center, 1973.

McCracken, J.B., ed. *Reducing Stress in Young Children's Lives.* NAEYC. Washington DC.

McGoldrick, M., Pierce, J. and Giordano, J. *Ethnicity and Family Therapy.* New York: The Guilford Press, 1982.

Montessori, M. *M. Montessori's Own Handbook.* New York: Schocken Books, 1970.

Riley, S.S. *How to Generate Values in Young Children: Integrity, Honesty, Individuality, Self-Confidence and Wisdom.* NAEYC. Washington DC.

Stone, J. *A Guide to Discipline.* rev. NAEYC. Washington DC, 1978.

Turecki, S. and Tonner, L. *The Difficult Child.* New York: Bantam Books, 1985.

Learning Activities

The most effective ways of helping young children feel good about themselves and feel comfortable and at ease with their peers, relate directly to the kinds of interaction they have with adults and children around them. In order to understand how children feel and react, we as teachers must spend time watching and observing the children we work with, on a regular basis in a variety of activities and situations. We need to keep regular anecdotal records on the children in our class. These activities will help us support children's emotional and social development.

——1. Once a week, note children's behavior and movements, describing what you actually observe, not teacher opinion or judgement - comments are fine, but should be identified as such. Anecdotal records can be kept on cards or in a notebook. Each note should be identified as follows:

Name _____ Class _____ Child's age in Sept. _____

Date and Time _____

Observations _____

_____

_____

_____

a. In keeping the anecdotal records on the children in your class, note how they feel about themselves, how they learn to handle themselves during routines, and how they approach different activities.

b. Select a particular child and note how the child makes contacts with adults and with children. Note child's response to contacts initiated by others.

c. Based on your observations, make a short written evaluation of each child in the class in terms of the child's social and emotional development.

d. Make four observations of one child during a learning task, a routine task (mealtime, cleanup, arrival/dismissal), outdoor play, and free play, to observe his emotional and social adjustment.

e. Write a report describing the psychodynamics of the behavior of a child in class or a child you know.

——2. Based on your anecdotal records, use the principles of positive discipline to help children accept limits and routines. Keep records of specific situations, children's interactions, and their reactions to your use of the principles.

——3. Make a list of classroom jobs for children to do. Jobs could include putting out napkins, spoons, cups for food service, feeding pets, watering plants, delivering messages such as attendance, and washing paint brushes. There should be a job chart and jobs should be broken into sufficiently small units so there is a job for each child - one job is to set out napkins, one to set out cups, etc.

Jobs should be assigned on a rotating basis as part of a child's responsibility for his life within the group and never as a reward for behavior or as a way of indicating a particular concern on the part of the teacher. If jobs are used as a reward, they do not enhance children's sense of independence and inner strength. Their concern will be to get the job and so prove to themselves that the teacher likes them. If the jobs are part of the routines of the classroom, then children know they each have an important role in the life of the classroom.

——4. Identify and use a variety of children's stories that help children identify and better understand their own and others' feelings.

a. Compile a bibliography of books that deal with children's feelings. List for each book: Subject (such as fear, anger, jealousy, finding a friend), Title, Illustrator and Publisher, Summary of book, Activities motivated by book. (See page 34)

b. Work out some activities that can develop from children's stories, such as making a rumpus as in *Where The Wild Things Are.*

——5. Identify and play in class, group games that do not have winners. Record children's reactions.

——6. Identify, *change*, and play in class group games that originally are played to win. Observe and record children's reactions.

——7. With the children, develop routines and rules to cover use of equipment and materials.

a. Together, help the children develop a list of "do's" for riding on the bus.

b. Identify and review with the children on an ongoing basis the sequence of routines in the classroom so children can predict "what's next" and can internalize the routines.

If you are working towards a Bilingual Specialization:
——8. Use both languages in helping children understand and deal with routines and classroom rules.

——9. Be aware of the different family and cultural expectations for children's behavior and incorporate these understandings in developing appropriate standards and expectations for children in the classroom.

Other related resources and Activities
(fill in your own resources)

_____

_____

_____

_____

_____

_____

_____

_____

Competency Goal IV

TO ESTABLISH POSITIVE AND PRODUCTIVE RELATIONSHIPS WITH FAMILIES

Functional
11. Families

The more we work with and observe young children as they learn about the world around them, the more we realize how important to their future development are these early years. Teachers, and in the classrooms they run, play a vital part in this development, but teachers in classrooms are certainly not the first adults with whom children come in contact. Children are learning from the very first moment they are born and from everyone and everything with whom they come in contact. The first people they get to know are their primary caregivers (parents, prandparents, step-parents, etc.) and other primary caregivers of infants and babies are their very first teachers. Children's first thoughts about themselves and their world comes through their interaction with these first caregivers.

We need to be well aware of the importance of the role these primary caregivers play, knowing that children bring with them the sum total of all their experiences with their families as they enter school. We have a two-fold responsibility to the parents and primary caregivers of the children we teach: to communicate with them and to help them develop their role as the first teachers of the children.

Young children form very strong relationships with their teachers. As good teachers, we should try to be as accepting, loving, and supportive as we can, and children will respond with love and trust. But it is hard for children to realize that they can love more than one person at a time, and they have already formed strong feelings relationships with members of their families. Although they can't talk about it, they often worry about these feelings of love they have for their teachers. They feel as if they are taking something away from their parents or caregivers. They worry about to do if parents and teachers don't agree, or worse yet, don't seem to like and accept each other? The children's sense of conflicting loyalties is bad enough - what if these are reflected and reinforced by problems that develop between their teachers and their parents and family members? Children then are torn and the resulting tension and conflict make it hard, even impossible, to learn and develop in the classroom.

If we are intent on enhancing children's healthy development, we must make sure that we maintain consistent open two-way communication with parents and primary caregivers, a free flow of information about their children's lives at home and at school. We need to understand and respect families' concerns and expectations for their children. We need to identify with parents' sense of vulnerability where children are concerned. When we compliment and

80

praise children to their parents and primary caregivers, they feel that they, too, are being praised. They have done a good job in producing and raising their children. When we criticize, condemn or reject a child, parents and primary caregivers take these feelings as being directed against them as well, because their children are a part of them. Teachers who are aware of these feelings can deal with them effectively in a variety of ways.

First, we need to be as accepting of the families as we are of the children. We need to be aware of and understand the diversity of ethnic and cultural backgrounds among our families and use this diversity to enrich the lives of everyone in the center. We need to avoid criticism or sarcasm. Then, we must admit to the reality of parental feelings by identifying with them from the beginning (through home or school visits before school opens, if possible), understanding that we all share one major concern - the well-being and continued healthy development of the children. We must build a relationship with families based on mutual trust. From the first days of school our communications must be frequent and factual and show that we understand and accept the needs of parents and other primary caregivers - we should be easy to reach and to talk to. Our requests should be realistic, and most important of all, we need to demonstrate our own obvious interest and acceptance of the children. We should consistently share interesting and positive information with families, information that is factual, simple, and important because it concerns the children. As we develop this positive, open-ended communication with families, we will have a pathway to share all aspects of children's development, usually positive, but sometimes identifying needs and concerns. All too often, schools communicate with families only to report accidents or children's negative behavior. No wonder parents are afraid of schools and teachers feel that parents don't like or trust them.

We also need to remember that when adults come to school in the role of parents, they are forcibly reminded of their own past roles as students in school. All too often, their reactions are based on their own, not very happy, school experiences. We must, therefore, help all our families understand that together we share a real love and concern for the well-being and education of their children and that, regardless of past experiences, together we can build a mutually supportive relationship that can support the children we all care for.

The second major responsibility we teachers have towards parents and primary caregivers is to help them fulfill their role as the first and most important teachers of their own children and to help them learn how to maintain a positive involvement in their children's education.

Children are learning from the moment of birth and we must help parents and families understand and enjoy their children and develop skills in helping them grow, learn, and develop to their fullest potential. We need to help parents and primary caregivers develop appropriate expectations for their children and learn to accept them and appreciate their strengths and meet their needs effectively. We must help families understand that they have an active part to play in supporting and furthering their children's education by keeping them aware of what children are learning, how they learn, and the kinds of ways they can support this learning outside of school. It is important that we help families realize that this involvement with their children's education should last throughout their child's school years.

Functional Area 11

Family Checklist *

Developing Communication and Trust

There are many ways for us, as teachers, to develop and maintain a relationship with families that is based on trust and awareness of the common deep concern about the children we both care for.

——1. We are aware that families and primary caregivers need to be reassured that they are welcome, accepted, and valued just as we welcome, accept, and value the children. We know that:

☐ Parents and primary caregivers have someone at the school/center to relate to and whom they can reach easily.

☐ There is a place for families in establishing communication.

☐ The center provides interesting and useful parenting information.

☐ Parents' and families' goals and expectations for their children may not be the same as those of the center. Differences are openly discussed and hopefully resolved. Ethnic and cultural differences are acknowledged and respected.

☐ All communications from families are accepted.

——2. We start the school year by reaching out to families to share with them the coming year of teaching and learning together with the staff and children. As teachers, we should:

☐ Help parents and primary caregivers feel welcome to visit school at any time.

☐ Make home visits, planning these carefully with social worker, if necessary and possible.

☐ Offer parents and primary caregivers specific information about school life to help them know what to expect.

☐ Arrange for parents, primary caregivers, and children to visit the school in small groups to pick out child's buddy, borrow a book. Offer refreshments.

☐ Share with families our awareness of their different cultures, values, beliefs, and practices.

——3. Whenever possible, we will stagger opening days so all children do not start at once.

☐ Parents and primary caregivers are encouraged to stay themselves or provide a supportive relative for the first days of school if needed.

☐ Teachers maintain close contact during the first week by phone, note, or word of mouth to reassure parents and primary caregivers about child's adjustment.

*This checklist may be copied for your portfolio.

——4. We are aware that children's coping with separation from home is closely related to how they trust the world in general and is a matter of real concern to their families.

☐ Make provisions for easy separation schedules for the first days of school.

☐ Reassure children that their parents or primary caregivers will be back or that they are going home right after lunch, nap, etc.

☐ Explain to the parent or primary caregiver each child's need for reassurance.

☐ Give family practical ideas to help with separation, such as a favorite toy or something of the parent's or primary caregiver's to hold, being sure that the parent or special caregiver keeps their word to child.

——5. As teachers, we initiate all family contacts in a positive way, being accepting, pleasant, and glad to interact with parents.

☐ We welcome all parental or primary caregiver visits with a smile and one-to-one conversation, however brief.

——6. We share all good news with families formally and informally on a regular basis as a foundation for mutual trust.

☐ Sharing is done verbally, by picture, newsletter, and informal notes.

☐ We share with families our affection for the child by voice, attitude, concern - all the little things that mean so much.

——7. We keep in touch with both child and parent or primary caregiver by means of notes or phone calls, if child is absent or ill. The family and child should be contacted the first day the child is absent.

——8. We use our own and the school's resources to maintain awareness of family needs and work cooperatively and realistically with parents and primary caregivers to meet child's needs. For example: We might say: "Mrs. S. helps as much as she can; it's hard for her at home right now." Not,"She can't be bothered." We:

☐ Try to ask parents and primary caregivers for reasonable contributions and look to them as a resource.

☐ Be aware that parental and family needs must sometimes be met before parents or primary caregivers can be concerned with the education of a three- or four-year-old.

☐ Consider family involvement in relation to family situations.

☐ Work with all the staff to plan meetings that are meaningful to families. Meetings should be related to children's activities; where families can voice concerns and gain information of real value.

☐ Extend the sense of open communication to the children's families by opening visitation to grandparents, siblings, step-family members, uncles, aunts, etc., when possible.

——9. We maintain records of home visits, conferences, and contacts with families to be aware of needs, concerns, and positive interactions with each family involved.

If we are competent as a Bilingual Specialist:

——10. We make every attempt to facilitate communication with families for whom English is not the native language by:

☐ Using common phrases connected to daily living bilingually - names of food, greetings, etc.

☐ Using an interpreter at school or on the phone in communication with families.

☐ Using signs and displays in parents' own language.

☐ Sending home notes and communications in bilingual or tri-lingual form as needed.

☐ Showing by our manner the desire to understand. An accepting attitude will communicate itself to the children and their parents. Incorporating important elements of the cultural background of the families of the children in the program, such as using food celebrations common to the cultural background of families in the nutrition program and in class activities.

——11. We work with bilingual families to identify the most effective ways of helping children develop communication skills.

Helping Families Support Their Own Children's Education

A major responsibility of all of us who teach young children is to help parents and primary caregivers understand and fulfill their role as the first and most important teachers of their own children.

——1. We work with parents to share with them the educational and developmental goals of the program. As teachers we:

☐ Have resource materials on education and development of young children.

☐ Work with all staff to arrange for parents to visit and participate when they can.

☐ Make time to talk with parents before and after a visit or observation.

☐ Introduce visiting parent to all staff when appropriate.

☐ Help parents plan for birthdays, trips, and other events important to their own children, encouraging participation by flexible time scheduling when necessary.

☐ Be aware of the use of audiovisual aids to help parents learn more about their child's activities in class.

——2. Provide families with information about the values of good early childhood education by audiovisual materials, classroom participation, and workshops.

☐ We work to develop parental awareness so their priorities for their children and the educational goals of the center are often quite close. For example: The teacher explains that children must learn to count concretely.

——3. We help parents and caregivers identify and expand their role as their child's first teacher by:

☐ Identifying for parents the many areas in which parents can enhance their children's lives by emotional support, intellectual activity, physical care. We must be specific in listing these ideas.

☐ Explaining that learning is a developmental process and helping parents and caregivers understand how children learn.

☐ Identifying for parents specific activities they can do with children or places they can go together.

——4. We always respond to parents' concerns about children's learning, growing, and development with understanding and acceptance by:

☐ Helping parents and caregivers understand the center's handling of a child and his needs.

☐ Offering information when asked on concerns important to parents. For example: We say, "Yes, of course you want John to read and these are ways we help him get ready."

☐ Helping parents to meet common needs and try to solve problems by telling them of supportive people and agencies in the community.

☐ Working with staff to plan regular conferences with parents at their convenience.

——5. We recognize and use the strengths and talents of families so they can contribute to the development of their own children and enrich the program of the group. We:

☐ Invite parents and primary caregivers to become part of the governing board of the center, the parent advisory board, or the parent-teacher group.

☐ All year long, invite parents and primary caregivers to use their skills in class to make and repair equipment, find materials, etc.

☐ Invite parents and primary caregivers to go on trips, conduct special activities like cooking, etc.

☐ Invite parents and primary caregivers to share special experiences and talents with children.

——6. As teachers we should work with parents to help them learn to make schools work for them to provide good education for their children in preschool and as the children move into the regular school system. We do this by:

☐ Helping parents and primary caregivers learn to identify needed resources in community through center staff and her contacts.

☐ Helping parents and primary caregivers learn to comply with justified preschool demands.

Resources

The following reading resources will be useful in providing help and information in working effectively with families and bringing about close and supportive relationships between the home and preschool center. Talk with fellow staff members or an early childhood specialist to help you select one or two readings you will find most helpful.

Parent Involvement in Preschool

Caplan, F. and Caplan, T. *Power of Play*. New York: Doubleday, 1974.

Catalado, C. *Parent Education for Early Childhood: Child Rearing Concepts and Program Content for the Practicing Professional*. New York: Teachers College, Columbia Univ., 1987.

Craft, D.J. *Parents and Teachers: A resource book for home, school and community relations*. Belmont, California: Wadsworth, 1979.

Duff, R.E., Ph.D., et al. *Building Successful Parent-Teacher Partnerships*. Atlanta: Humanics Limited.

Galinsky, E. *The Six Stages of Parenthood*. Mass: Addison-Wesley Publishing, 1987.

Honig, A. *Parent Involvement in Early Childhood Education*. NAEYC. Washington DC.

Hymes, J. *Effective Home School Relations*. rev. California: South Carolina Assoc. for the Education of Young Children, 1974.

Mussen, Conger and Kagen. *Child Development and Personality*. New York: Harper & Row, 1974.

Read, K. *The Nursery School: Human Relations and Learning*. 6th ed. Chap. 20 Philadelphia, W.B. Saunders, 1976.

Riley, Mary Tom. *LATON - The Parent Book.* Atlanta: Humanics Limited, 1977.

Stevens, J. and Matthews, M., ed. *Mother/Child Father/Child Relationships.* NAEYC. Washington DC, 1978.

Stone, J.G. *Teacher Parent Relationships.* NAEYC. Washington DC, 1987.

Turecki, S. and Tonner, L. *The Difficult Child.* New York: Bantam Books, 1985.

U.S. Dept. of HEW-OCD. *Parent Involvement.* Head Start Rainbow Series OEO #6108-12

U.S. Dept. of HEW-OCD. *Volunteers.* Head Start Rainbow Series OCD 72-49

Warner and Guill. *Beautiful Junk.* Washington, D.C. DHEW-OCD publ.#73-1036

Warren, R.M. *Caring, Supporting Children's Growth.* NAEYC. Washington DC.

Williams, Doris, Ph.D. *Handbook for Involving Parents in Education.* Atlanta: Humanics Limited, 1985.

Wilson, Gary. *Parents and Teachers.* Atlanta: Humanics Limited, 1976.

Zavitkovsky, D. et al. *Listen to the Children.* NAEYC. Washington DC.

Note: See also readings in Competency III

Families as Their Own Children's Teachers

Brazelton, T.B. *Toddlers and Parents.* New York: Delacorte Press, 1974.

Castle, Kathryn. *The Infant & Toddler Handbook - Invitations for Optimum Early Development.* Atlanta: Humanics Limited, 1983.

Gordon, I. *Baby Learning Through Baby Play.* New York: St. Martins Press, 1970.

Gordon, I. *Child Learning Through Child Play.* New York: St. Martins Press, 1972.

Gordon and Kiester. *Parents Can Be Teachers.* College Park, Maryland: Head Start Regional Resource and Training Center.

Klein, Barry. *Lives of Families.* Atlanta: Humanics Limited, 1985.

LeShan, E. *When Your Child Drives You Crazy.* New York: St. Martins Press, 1985.

Miller, J. and Weissman, S. *The Parents' Guide to Day Care.* New York: Bantam Books, 1986.

Pulaski, M.A. *Your Baby's Mind and How It Grows: Piaget's Theory for Parents.* New York: Harper & Row, 1978.

Shiff, E., ed. *Experts Advise Parents: A Guide to Raising Loving, Responsible Children.* New York: Delacorte, 1974.

Smith, H. *Survival Handbook for the Preschool Mother.* Chicago: Follett Publ., 1987.

Sparling, J. and Lewis, J. *Learning Games for the First Three Years.* New York: Berkeley, 1983.

Sparling, J. and Lewis, J. *Learning Games for Threes and Fours.* New York: Berkeley, 1984.

Patterns of Family Living

Goldrich, M., Pierce, M. and Giordano, J. *Ethnicity and Family Therapy.* New York: The Guilford Press, 1982.

Howard, A.E. *The American Family: Myth and Reality.* NAEYC. Washington DC.

Saracho, O. and Spodek, B. *Understanding the Multicultural Experience in Early Childhood Education.* NAEYC. Washington DC.

Schmidt, V. and McNEill, E. *Cultural Awareness, A Resource Bibliography.* NAEYC. Washington DC.

Wallerstein, J.S. and Kelly, J. *Surviving the Break-up: How Children and Parents Cope With Divorce.* New York: Basic Books, 1983.

Learning Activities

Carrying out some of the following learning activities will help your improve your skills in developing supportive and cooperative activities and feelings between teachers and parents.

——1. List ways to help parents become more involved in and aware of their children's activities in school. Identify why you feel it is important to encourage parent involvement.

——2. Plan and carry out some of the ideas listed in No. 1.

——3. Try, by talking with parents, to identify a need common to all parents in the center.

——4. Conduct a workshop based on some need (see No. 3 above). Arrange for this workshop to be observed by a specialist or advisor and evaluated in terms of effectiveness in reaching and influencing parents.

——5. Plan and carry out parent workshops based on the following:

    a. What a child learns through free play activities.

    b. Ways to carry on learning activities started at school.

    c. Ideas of positive discipline.

——6. Keep a log of any activities or plans carried out with parents, including home visits, etc.

——7. Outline plans for the first days of school with reasons for these plans. Describe how planning for the first days of school relate to parents involvement, making parents and children feel comfortable and helping to develop mutual sense of trust.

——8. Investigate how different programs plan for the first days of school.

——9. Produce, with parents when possible, a newsletter for your class. Keep track of any parent-initiated contact resulting from this activity.

——10. Using the information from readings and personal experiences, make a list of ways in which family life and problems of parental attitudes influence the education of young children.

——11. Make a case study of a child who is or has been in the classroom, identifying some of the family and community forces that have influenced the child's adjustment and development in the preschool classroom.

——12. Identify, describe, and try to carry out specific ways for parents to become involved in their children's education. Keep a record of any parents' and children's reactions to these activities.

——13. Build a file of at-home activities. Prepare materials to help children develop specific concepts and establish a toy lending library arrangement for parents to use these with their children. Note any children's and/or parents' reactions to these activities.

——14. Establish a simple-to-run class lending library to help parents establish habits of reading to children on a regular basis. Note children's and parents' reactions.

Other Related Learning Resources and Activities
(Fill in your own resources.)

_____

_____

_____

_____

_____

_____

_____

_____

_____

_____

_____

_____

_____

_____

_____

_____

_____

_____

Competency Goal V

TO ENSURE A WELL-RUN, PURPOSEFUL PROGRAM, RESPONSIVE TO PARTICIPANTS' NEEDS

In order to respond to other people, we as professionals must be aware of how they think and feel. We can borrow from children their habit of steady, careful observation of those with whom they live and work. We need to watch and see how children handle themselves, interact with others, and approach new experiences, and so learn about their strengths and needs. We should be able to record the information we gain so we can share our insights with other staff members and effectively meet children's needs and enhance their development. As ongoing records of children's behavior help us understand them better and react more effectively to them, these same records become a record of children's growth. We need to react to children where they are now and not just on the basis of past outgrown behaviors. Also, we often can forget the children's past developmental activities as they no longer apply to them. As a result we may not have any basis for evaluating growth and change in the children over a period of time. "Oh yes, he plays with others just fine," we say, no longer concerned with and thus forgetting the child's struggle to live cooperatively with his/her peers. Only as we re-read our anecdotal records of children's behavior can we trace the child's patterns of development. Teachers who have recorded information on children's growth and development also have a great deal of relevant information that can help other people work effectively with the children to meet special needs.

Whatever they do and whoever they do it with, children are learning all the time by watching, observing, and interacting with their environment. They learn as they watch how their teachers interact with each other, with other children, and with the other adults who make up the community of the school. As teachers of young children, we need to develop our skills in planning with fellow staff, visitors, and volunteers to maintain a good learning environment and provide appropriate learning activities. Then each of us working in the classroom understands our roles and responsibilities, routines and learning activities go smoothly. Children do not waste their time waiting, we are relaxed and can respond to children and each other sharing a mutual enjoyment in each other and the work we do. Just as we accept and support children in our classes, we must accept and support all our fellow staff members. We must remember that children tend to treat others as they themselves are treated, and this is true of adults, too. A climate that is relaxed and accepting will produce a good "growing" environment for adults and children alike.

A well-planned, smoothly functioning learning environment for young children depends on the effectiveness with which all of us who are involved can fulfill our different functions.

We also need to be aware of fellow staff members' responsibilities and help to maintain the program organization as we understand all of its aspects, in addition to our own individual classroom functions.

NOTE: The Humanics National Child Assessment Form is an excellent checklist for recording children's behavior. It, and many other helpful record-keeping forms, can be ordered through Humanics, P.O.Box 7447, Atlanta, GA. 30309

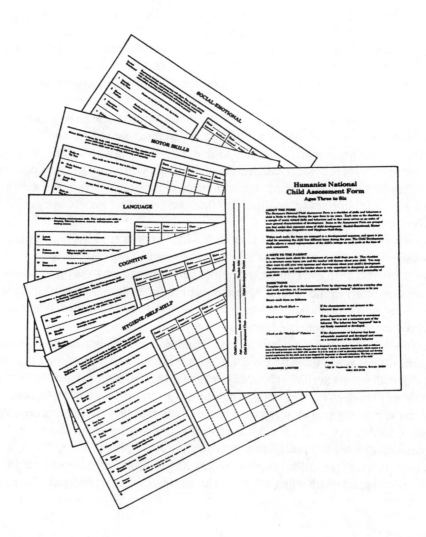

Functional Area 12

Program Management Checklist*

—1. As teachers of young children, we try to learn as much as we can about the growth and developmental needs of the children in our classes. We:

☐ Keep dated anecdotal records on each child on a regular basis for the whole year, keeping careful records of child's behavior during this period.

☐ Be aware of each child's developmental level and areas of growth.

☐ Use some form of checklist to determine for each child some basic skill levels and emotional and social behavior at the start of the year and as the months pass.

☐ Keep a few examples of art work, 3 to 4 per year, labeled with child's name and date for the purposes of observing development.

☐ Try not to form any preconceived ideas about any child. For example: "Watch out for that Smith kid." "None of that family ever reads well."

—2. On the basis of these anecdotal records, we become aware of and can assess special needs of individual children and call in a specialist's help when needed. We are:

☐ Aware of child's patterns of behavior from the first days of school by keeping regular observations.

☐ Aware of growth or change in the child or lack of growth.

☐ Aware that real lack of growth over several months may indicate problems and we are able to comment based on observations. For example: Records show that a child continues poor adaptive behavior, and substitutes one unacceptable behavior for another, or always seems tense and worried.

☐ Aware when child's behavior is not consistent with broad developmental norms.

☐ Aware when a child's behavior is inappropriate. For example: Child laughs when his feelings are very hurt or never shows affection for anyone.

☐ Aware when a child does not function in any way on a level with the class.

☐ Willing to ask for other opinions and find the right people to whom concerns can be expressed.

—3. With support from the director and others, if necessary, share concerns with parents and ask if they see any problem. (This will *not* be the first time we talk to parents.) We are:

☐ Aware of the need to express concerns carefully and in a supportive manner with parents.

*This checklist may be copied for your portfolio.

——4. We are able to identify school and community resources that can help us meet the needs of individual children and families when necessary. We can talk with other staff who offer special services about children with problems and needs.

——5. We establish and maintain warm mutually supportive and always professional relationships with fellow staff members and classroom co-workers. We:

☐ Talk regularly with co-teacher/aide about the children in class, using observations to describe behavior.

☐ Talk regularly with co-teacher/aide about the group as a whole and how it functions. See that all adults give full attention to children during school hours.

☐ Are honest in dealing with personality conflicts among staff and seek the assistance of the supervisor in solving them.

☐ Treat all staff members with respect.

☐ Share positive events with other staff. For example: When a child shows evidence of growth.

☐ Are aware of the need to keep classrooms covered in terms of supervision and share this responsibility with staff as a whole.

——6. We are aware of the need to plan cooperatively with co-workers to ensure a smoothly running classroom. We can do this by:

☐ discussing daily/weekly/monthly plans with fellow staff members.

☐ Planning jointly with other staff members for special trips, etc.

☐ Planning jointly with other staff members to meet emergencies, such as no food, lack of heat, etc.

☐ Involving self and staff in workshops, school visits, to learn to use new materials and new methods, etc.

☐ Sharing new professional ideas, workshops, etc., with other staff members.

☐ Giving family members, visitors, and volunteers guidance in their work in the classroom - what their duties are, what sort of behavior they can expect, etc.

——7. As teachers we are aware of how the center functions in terms of the ordering of supplies and equipment, scheduling of staff time, including all paraprofessionals and volunteers. We can plan and share cooperatively to maintain a well-run center by sharing and planning with responsible staff members or specialists.

——8. We are aware of how food and transportation services are provided in the program and of special needs that may arise from day to day.

——9. We work with health staff of center to meet physical and emotional needs of children. We will:

☐ Note problems with children's clothing needs and communicate with appropriate staff.

☐ Note problems concerning signs of physical or sexual abuse or maltreatment and how to report such problems.

☐ Be aware of signs of physical illness in children and communicate these with health aide.

☐ Be aware of signs and indications of special physical, intellectual, or emotional handicaps and share our concerns with the appropriate staff members.

——10. We are aware of the need for usable forms:

☐ Child evaluation forms that are non-judgmental.

☐ Home visit forms.
☐ Anecdotal record forms.
—11. We make our own materials, trying to get what is needed for the program from all reasonable sources.
—12. Be aware of methods of identifying and ordering supplies and equipment and have access to and identify equipment catalogues. We are:
☐ Aware of appropriate materials for the indoor and outdoor learning environments.
☐ Aware of reasons for purchasing different kinds of equipment.
☐ Aware of children's different needs for equipment and supplies based on age levels.
☐ Aware of equipment and supplies that may be needed for the education of the exceptional child.
—13. Our understanding of the elements of good classroom management are indicated by:
☐ A well-organized and maintained classroom (Competency Goal 1).
☐ Cooperatively, clearly planned, and balanced daily program with effective use of time and active and quiet activities.
☐ Reasonable expectations for children's behavior in terms of attention span, need for concrete experiences, etc.
☐ Observably smooth transitions and control, based on good interpersonal relationships with all children.
—14. We provide a well-organized and maintained room as described in Functional Area 3, Learning Environment.
—15. We plan any lessons or demonstrations always using teaching techniques appropriate for the way young children learn.
☐ Demonstrations allow for children to try for themselves immediately. For example: "I'll peel my egg, while you peel yours."
☐ Demonstrations are done in small groups so children are not only learning from the demonstration but improving their attention skills. Group is small so children do not learn to tune out.
☐ Demonstrations and instruction with the total group are short and involve each child individually.
—16. We deal effectively with differences in children's style and pace of learning by:
☐ Presenting group teaching-learning activities so children can participate at their individual levels of involvement. Children cut their own eggs, plant their own seeds, and work with one other child to experiment with water pressure.
☐ Organizing materials and equipment so that cleanup is a constant exercise in classification and ordering skills.
☐ Offering most learning opportunities for children by activities planned for individual participation. Children are involved in well-planned interest centers. Children do not observe, they do it themselves.
☐ Offering children the opportunity to plan some activities for themselves since they have a variety of materials to choose from. For example: Adequate number and assortment of blocks, etc.

☐ Providing one-to-one awareness and support of children as staff moves about the room.

☐ Planning so children can repeat activities as they choose, based on their own developmental needs.

☐ Offering a range of cultural activities reflecting the backgrounds of children in the center.

—17. We balance children's use of unstructured materials like paint, clay, and blocks with structured materials that require specific procedures and skills, balancing the use of activities that encourage exploration and independent discovery with teaching and demonstrating.

☐ Unstructured materials, such as paint, blocks, sand, water, and clay, are available to children on a regular basis, in the context of a free choice period.

☐ Structured materials requiring specific procedures and skills are available on a regular basis. For example: Manipulative toys requiring small muscle skills, opportunities to tear, cut, etc.

☐ Teachers support children's involvement by their attention and by keeping materials available and interesting.

☐ Teachers watch children to see if they are ready for additional stimulation. For example: Children do not use equipment or area of interest after making good use of the area, etc., so new materials are added.

—18. We plan with adults and children to maintain a balanced daily program using time effectively:

☐ Daily program allows time for children to practice self-help skills and complete activities without rushing.

☐ Daily program allows for an adequate amount of time in free choice activities so children can work through special projects.

☐ Daily program allows time for children to understand and successfully carry out routines connected with eating, cleanup, toileting, sleeping, etc.

☐ Daily program provides for a daily free choice play period long enough to allow for gradually extended involvement of children in their own activities depending on children's experience in play and ability to stay constructively involved.

☐ Daily program provides for an appropriate balance of active and quiet periods for children.

—19. We plan a clear, consistent routine and daily program by:

☐ Keeping program activities in the same sequence, especially for the first months of school.

☐ Planning carefully for the transition periods in the day so each staff member has internalized the routines and the sequence of the day.

☐ Planning carefully for special events and changes by structuring the staff members so each one know their responsibilities.

☐ Parents and volunteers in the classroom are also made aware of their own responsibilities.

☐ Planning routines carefully and explaining clearly so children find it easy to understand routines and follow them.

☐ Patterns for routines and transitions are set the first days of school, clearly and gently, with the routines explained step by step. Important routines are: eating, cleanup, toileting, use of materials, transportation, and rest (if necessary).

☐ Explanations about routines are repeated regularly with no blame attached to children or anyone who might forget.

☐ Any changes in routines are clearly explained to the children.

☐ Children are given chances to verbalize their knowledge of the routines.

☐ Children are told about special events of the day. Special activities, such as trips, are integrated into normal daily routines with as little disruption as possible. For example: Birthday party is part of snack or lunch time; trip is part of outdoor activity time.

☐ Changes are not talked about so far in advance that they are beyond children's awareness of the passage of time.

☐ Children are alerted to teachers' absences. They also know that teachers will return.

☐ If you are working towards a Bilingual Specialization, you will:

—20. Be aware of the needs of children and families of different cultural backgrounds and share your understanding with other staff members.

—21. Respond to families' concerns about culturally-based differences in language, adult/child interactions, and educational goals.

—22. Identify and use a variety of bicultural materials relating to children's development and to parenting skills.

Resources

The following reading resources cover many aspects of program management and program planning in schools for young children. Your advisor, early childhood specialist, supervisor, director, or fellow staff member can help you select ones that are appropriate.

Abbott-Shim, Martha, Ph.D. *The Child Care Inventory Administration Manual.* Atlanta: Humanics Limited, 1986.

Boressof, T. *Children, The Early Childhood Classroom and You.* New York: ECEC.

Brown, J., ed. *Administering Programs for Young Children.* NAEYC. Washington DC.

Butler, A. *Early Childhood Education, Planning and Administering Programs.* New York: Van Nostrand, 1974.

Butler, Gotts, and Ginsenberry. *Early Childhood Education: Developmental Objectives and Individualized Approach.* Ohio: Charles Merrill, 1975.

Cherry, Harkness, and Kuzma. *Nursery School and Day Care Center Management Guide.* California: Fearon Pitman, 1978.

Elkind, D. *Miseducation Preschoolers at Risk.* New York: A. Knopf, 1987.

Hildebrand, V. *Guiding Young Children.* New York: MacMillan, 1975.

Hirsh, V. *Transitions.* New York: ECEC of New York City, 1972.

Hohlmann, M., Banet, B. and Weikart, D. *Young Children in Action: A Manual for Preschool Educators.* Ypsilanti, Michigan: The High/Scope Press, 1979.

Lorton, John and Walley, Bertha. *The Administrator's Handbook for Child Care Providers.* Atlanta: Humanics Limited.

Merrill, B. *Learning about Teaching from Children.* New York: RAEYC, 1984.

Pitcher, E. *Helping Young Children Learn.* 3rd ed. Ohio: Charles Merrill, 1979.

Read, K., Gardner, B. and Mahler, P. *Early Childhood Programs: A Laboratory for Human Relationships.* 8th ed. New York: Holt, Rinehart & Winston, 1986.

Resource Guides, NAEYC: Washington, D.C.
Programs for 4-Year-Olds
Child Care Center Diseases and Sick Child Care
Computers and Young Children
Rudolph, M. *From Hand to Head.* New York: McGraw Hill, 1973.
Seefeld, C. *Early Childhood Curriculum: A Review of Current Research.* New York: Teachers College Press, Columbia University, 1986.
Smith, Carol. *Better Meetings.* Atlanta: Humanics Limited, 1975.
Souweine, J., Crimmins, S. and Mazel, C. *Mainstreaming Ideas for Teaching Young Children.* NAEYC. Washington DC, 1981.
Spodek, B. *Handbook of Research in Early Childhood Education.* New York: Free Press, 1982.

Learning Activities
Carrying out some of the following learning activities will help you develop skills in effective program organization and management.
—1. Develop a written plan of daily program with reasons for the sequence of activities. Use information gained from the readings.
—2. Keep a daily log of the sequence of routines. Note problems, your own feelings of pressure, relaxation, etc. Plan to improve your routines and discuss these plans with fellow staff.
—3. Keep daily lesson plans, noting special activities and routines, indicating daily program and routines and the special activities planned for each week.
—4. Observe your classroom and list self-help activities for children that you have to put into practice in your room.
—5. Develop a written monthly curriculum framework listing educational goals for each month and activities to help achieve these goals on a weekly basis.

The following learning activities will help us function effectively as members of a teaching staff.
—1. Keep a log of the interaction between yourself and your co-worker, noting instances of cooperation, joint plans or activities that did or didn't work.
—2. Identify goals for inter-staff relationships.
—3. Write up guidelines for volunteers to use in the classroom.
—4. Discuss with co-workers and then write up, directions for bus routines, class routines, etc.
—5. Develop a teacher's resource file in which you organize and keep information gained from past experiences and training that will be helpful to you in your work. This activity also helps you develop and maintain a sense of professionalism and identify and use resources and information already collected.
—6. Identify some performance goals for staff in preschool program.
—7. Plan and carry out a workshop for staff based on identified goals or staff needs. Have early childhood specialist, teacher, or advisor attend and evaluate the workshop.
—8. Keep daily/weekly anecdotal records on children in the class, Use the records to identify children's needs, growth, etc.

Other Related Learning Resources and Activities
(Fill in your own resources.)

_____

_____

_____

_____

_____

_____

_____

_____

_____

_____

_____

_____

_____

_____

Competency Goal VI

TO MAINTAIN A COMMITMENT TO PROFESSIONALISM

Functional Area
13 Professionalism

To carry out the responsibilities of nurturing the growth and development of young children, we must have the needed knowledge, skill, understanding, and competencies.

It is supportive of our sense of professionalism, self-worth, and teacher effectiveness if, as we improve our teaching skills and get to know our own selves better, we also have a sense of our place in the history of preschool education. It always helps to know where we have been to better identify where we are going. We can benefit from an overview of the history of early education and awareness of current programs. Even if we have completed our studies of the competencies in early childhood education, it is important to maintain our commitment to our profession, to be aware of current information and research in the field of child development and early education.

Functional Area 13

Professional Checklist*

As competent and committed professionals in the field of early childhood education:

☐ We maintain contact with our colleagues through membership in professional organizations and contribute together, functioning to the best of our abilities.

☐ We attend inservice workshops and conferences.

☐ We share information and skills with our fellow staff members.

☐ We read professional journals and current materials, evaluating and utilizing the information to enhance our teaching skills.

☐ We work closely with fellow staff to enrich our own classrooms and the life at the center.

☐ We make ourselves aware of government issues relating to young children at the local, state, and federal level.

☐ We participate in evaluations of our programs, classrooms, and ourselves through self-assessment and as a joint staff activity.

Resources

As professionals in the field of early childhood education, we should maintain contact or membership in our professional organizations:

☐ Your local affiliate of the National Association for the Education of Young Children.

☐ Local and state organizations of: educators of young children, educators of special children, and educators of gifted children.

☐ As professional early childhood educators, we should read the professional journals concerned with children and with early childhood education such as:

☐ *Young Children* NAEYC**

☐ *Children Today* - Office of Human Development Services, Department of Health and Human Services, U.S. Government Printing Office, Washington, DC 20402

*This checklist may be copied for your portfolio.

**of particular interest to teachers in the field of early childhood education is "Professionalism of Early Childhood Educators."Mary Ann Radomski. Young Children. July, 1986. NAEYC. Washington DC.

The National Association for the Education of Young Children has developed an accreditation process for centers for young children. Professional staff who read and pursue this accreditation participate in a thorough self-study of their teaching and their program.

☐ National Academy of Early Childhood Programs, NAEYC.

☐ *Guide to Accreditation - Self-Study Validation, Accreditation 1985*

☐ The Children's Defense Fund, on a yearly basis, provides detailed information focusing on programs and policies that affect large numbers of children in the publication, A Children's Defense Budget 1989 - An Analysis of our Nation's Investment in Children. 122 C Street, NW, Washington, DC 20001

Learning Activities

To maintain and extend our sense of professionalism we can:

—1. Read an article, take notes, and share them with fellow staff.

—2. Attend a workshop and share our notes with fellow staff.

—3. Develop alone or with a fellow staff member, a workshop on a topic jointly selected by staff or parents.

—4. Preview professional materials in the areas of curriculum, child development, etc., to share with fellow staff.

—5. Develop a personal professional library organized on the basis of the competency areas.

—6. Participate in self-evaluation activities with program administrators or early childhood specialist.

Other Related Learning Resources and Activities
(Fill in your own resources.)

_____

_____

_____

_____

_____

_____

_____

_____

Conclusion

In an environment that supports their growth and development, children in general:

Work, play and talk freely and easily with adults and with each other.

Seem happy and relaxed, smile and laugh together.

Are busy in self-directed activities, neither too quiet or too controlled.

Seem calm and serene, with few arguments or tears.

I hope by sharing my ideas and experiences in working with young children and teachers, I can help you, the readers, improve your competencies working with young children. If children and teachers learn, grow, and enjoy their lives together, everyone benefits.

I hope this guide is useful to you. Add your own ideas, reading resources, reactions, and learning activities to the resources and activities listed here. Be happy teaching!

It's good to be sitting still,
And it's good to be running wild,
And it's good to be by yourself alone
Or with another child.
And whether the child's grown up,
Or whether the child is small,
So long as it really is a Child
It doesn't matter at all.

Joyce Lankester Brisley
Milly-Malley-Mandy Stories
George G. Harrap & Co., Inc.
London 1928.